WRECKS of the
MEDITERRANEAN

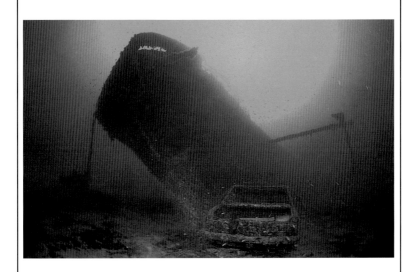

WHITE STAR
PUBLISHERS

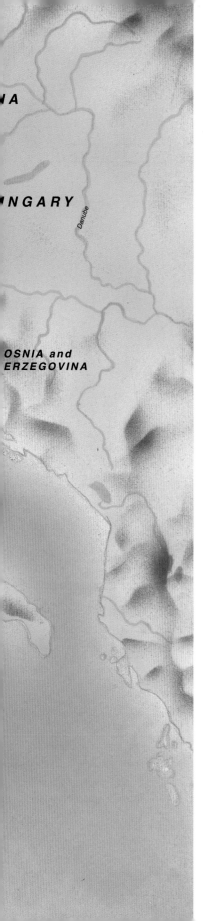

Contents

Texts and photographs
Kurt Amsler
Andrea Ghisotti
Roberto Rinaldi
Egidio Trainito

Editorial production
Valeria Manferto De Fabianis
Laura Accomazzo

Technical Consultance
Fabio Bourbon

Graphic design
Patrizia Balocco Lovisetti

Translation
Neil Frazer Davenport

The Publisher wishes to thank Gianni Berruti, Patrick Mouton, Lun Vanrell and Ruud Vroege for their valuable assistance.

The colour illustrations showing the wrecks are purely indicative and for greater clarity do not contain potentially confusing details such as fishing nets, cables, halyards etc.

1 - *The form of the ferry* Nasim II *which sank in 1976 off the island of Giannutri stands out sharply against the surface of the sea.*

© 2003 White Star srl
Via Candido Sassone 24
Vercelli, Italy
www.whitestar.it

ISBN 88-8095-728-7
REPRINTS:
1 2 3 4 5 6   07 06 05 04 03

Printed by C&C Offset Printing Co. LTD, China
Colour separations by Cliché Offset,
Milan, Italy.

INTRODUCTION

by Andrea Ghisotti

A

I remember my first wreck, and that emotional turmoil which was to accompany me so often over the following years, as clearly as if it was yesterday. I was 16 years old, I had no breathing gear of my own and had to borrow a friend's tanks when I dived. A few months earlier the *Mohawk Deer*, a large Canadian tanker, had gone down near Portofino, in Italy. It had been dashed to pieces during a memorable libecciata (a Mediterranean wind). The shattered stern section lay at a depth of just a few metres and I had already carefully examined it, tracing a plan of all the plates after many breath-holding dives. I now wanted to locate the forward section which ought to have been lying close by, but which I had not yet been able to find. Having explored the length of the coast, I eventually turned my attention to the deeper waters of the broad bay. I was young, but dived fairly well; after hyperventilating I dived head first and swam along the flat, pebbled sea-bed at a depth of around thirty metres. I had already turned ready to surface when my heart missed a beat. Just a few metres away, in the murky green half-light, appeared the huge, threatening flank of a ship, with the portholes and windows of the bridge staring at me like the empty eye sockets of a monstrous skull. What a shock! I shot to the surface as if chased by the hounds of hell, desperately swimming to my boat. For some time afterwards I lost all interest in that particular wreck. Many years on, I can look back on that irrational fear with a smile. I have now dived to that wreck dozens of times, day and night, in company and on my own. However, the experience does serve as an, albeit exaggerated, demonstration of the enormous emotional charge which can be generated by the sight of a large sunken vessel. These are unconscious fears, rooted in our childhood fantasies of fabled wrecks and adventures constructed around the stories we had read. I realise that not everybody feels

B

the same way about a wreck. For some a sunken ship may just be an inanimate, rusting hulk. For others it may be something magical and mysterious. Something which disappeared long ago and which has rematerialised and come back to life. A dive to the sea-bed where a new wreck lies waiting to be discovered, is like a trip through time and space which may take you back years or even decades. As you descend, peering through the increasingly dark and featureless water, in your mind's eye

A - A diver exploring the wreck of the KT *which sank in the waters off Sestri Levante on the Ligurian coast in the April of 1944. The vessel was struck by a torpedo launched by an allied submarine.*

B - The prow of the Mohawk Deer, *a tanker which sank close to Portofino (Liguria) on the 5th of November, 1967, is intact and is lying at a depth of 23 metres, with the highest parts at 16 metres from the surface.*

C - The submarine Rubis, *lying upright on the sea-bed, is a fascinating destination for the divers exploring the waters off Cap Camarat on the Côte d'Azure. In this shot you can see the open hatch which almost invites you to enter. In reality the passage is narrow and you would be ill-advised to enter.*

A

B

A - In this
photograph you
can see one of the
machine-guns
mounted on the
LST which sank in
February, 1943,
following a strong
mistral wind which
tore away the
vessel's moorings
and sent her on the
rocks of Punta Papa
close to the island
of Ponza.

B - The fuselage of
the Junkers Ju. 88,
clearly showing the
effects of the
corrosive action of
salt water, is lying
off the island of Le
Frioul, at a depth of
around 53 metres.

you begin running through the
images pieced together from the
information you have managed to
gather during your initial research,
and the archives and newspapers you
have scoured. Then, all of a sudden,
these images melt away like mist
before the sun as you gain your first
sight of the real thing, first no more
than a distant blur, but gradually
coming into focus and taking on
form. How can one possibly remain
indifferent at this point? I can
understand fear, at times it is nothing
less than terror, I can understand
curiosity, euphoria and perhaps
disappointment, but not indifference.
This book is dedicated to all those
who are fascinated by wrecks.
It contains 32 accounts of wrecks
lying at the bottom of the
Mediterranean; ships and planes of
the last two centuries. There is
nothing really old, therefore, and
those who have in mind a classic
cartoon image of a romantic Spanish
galleon dripping pieces of eight and
precious stones will perhaps be
disappointed. Neither is it the book
for those interested in ancient
remains. These belong to the realm
of pure archaeology and are out of
the range of private divers. Every
country protects its archaeological
heritage with specific laws almost
always forbidding diving over
archaeological sites or the removal of
relics, something that 90% of diving
"archaeologists" would like to do.
However, If you think about it, the
"modern" wrecks, those of the
nineteenth and twentieth centuries,
are actually those which provide
most interest for divers. Virtually

nothing remains of the wooden ships
constructed in earlier centuries. You
never come across a complete hull.
Steel and aluminium in the case of
aircraft, are very resistant materials,
and even though corrosion may have
set in the structure will remain
unaltered for many years. This has
given rise to a new branch of
archaeology, that of modern relics,
which is no less enthralling than that
concerned with earlier times. Many
of the wrecks are still waiting for their
story to be told. Exploring a wreck
and then spending hours in archives
or libraries trying to reconstruct
events, dates and names which
seldom match up is a satisfying
hobby. It is a veritable treasure hunt.
As with all long and difficult searches,
each small step forwards is a reward
in itself. You do not necessarily have
to explore new wrecks and begin
your research from scratch. Each
wreck described in this guide can be
"rediscovered" by the reader in all
its myriad details. You can immerse
yourself in this branch of modern
archaeology, learning to recognise
the structural features of ships and
planes.
Of the 32 wrecks described in this
book, over half sank during the
First and Second World Wars.
A enthusiasm for history now comes
into play, encouraged by a desire to
know more about why there are so
many wrecks in particular areas, all
linked to the same historical period.
The forms of certain boats like the
German barges, or the LST, may be
representative of the specific
demands of a certain era. It is equally
fascinating to study the evolution of
naval architecture which allows us to
date wrecks with a certain degree of
precision. The ships of the late
nineteenth and early twentieth
centuries had vertical prows.
Increasingly inclined prows were
introduced as the years passed.
Propellers, rudders, engine-room
gear, boilers, funnels and
superstructure also evolved in a
similar fashion. Divers examining
wrecks must develop one faculty
above all others, that of observation.
A free dive, suspended a few metres
above a wreck will be far more
informative than a premature
exploration of its interior. Many divers
visit wrecks for years without being

able to tell you whether the anchors are still in place or not. Try instead to absorb every detail and, as soon as you surface, to jot down a sketch of the wreck. You will be surprised at how much information you missed, but in successive dives you will become increasingly observant and precise. Research and understanding is always the best way of getting into a subject. Unfortunately however, there are divers who see a wreck as a terrain of conquest. Relics are there to be removed, portholes to be dismantled. This is uncivil behaviour, and these individuals have understood nothing of the appeal of a wreck, they obviously have no love for it or they would not destroy it. There is no sense in taking away "mementoes" which almost always end up rusting away forgotten in a cellar. It is above all selfish as it deprives other divers of the joy of seeing those objects in situ. I hope that the mentality of these vandals changes quickly and that this huge, fantastic heritage can be preserved for future generations.

C - Wrecks are often the subjects of studies and research, not only from a historical point of view. After even a brief period underwater they are colonised by an incredible variety of marine organisms, and numerous fish choose to take up residence among these "artificial rocks". In this shot you see the wreck of the Santa Lucia, a mail-boat which sank on the 10th of July, 1943 following an attack by a squadron of torpedo bombers.

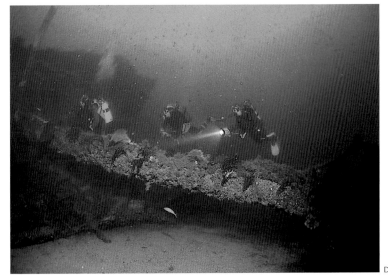

D - Numerous multi-coloured gorgonians grow on parts of the Sagona, a freighter which sank off the island of Porquerolles on the 3rd of December, 1945.

E - The American-built Wildcat was a carrier-borne fighters of the Second World War. They were also used by the Royal Navy, and this one, which carries British markings, is lying at 53 metres off Formigue du Lavandou.

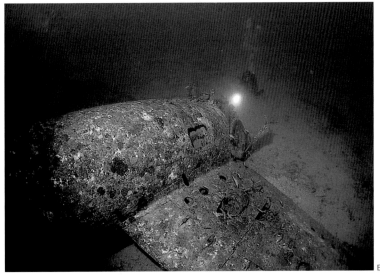

When you go diving in tropical waters, the organization of the dives, the boat and all the underwater activities, including the location of the diving sites, is generaly delegated to local diving centres or the crew of the charter boat on which you are spending your holiday. There is therefore no need to have specialised knowledge of the area, the charts, the instrumentation and the techniques of searching for a wreck. In these cases you very often dive without even knowing exactly where you are. Things are rather different in the Mediterranean where, at least in Italy, diving centres have only recently been established and are not evenly distributed along the coasts. Moreover, divers in home waters often have their own boats, and so have to locate the diving sites themselves and organize all aspects of the dive, including the mooring of the boat, and finding it again at the end of the dive. In this situation you need specialised knowledge, not only of diving techniques, but also of navigation, chart reading and the use of echo-sounders and electronic instrumentation. A healthy dose of the mariner's art comes in handy too. The search for a wreck very often begins on a nautical chart on which sunken vessels are marked with a symbol consisting of a horizontal dash intersected by three shorter perpendicular strokes. On Italian charts, if the wreck is covered by less than 18 metres of water the symbol is surrounded by a dotted line. There are three fundamental techniques for finding this point on the open sea. The first consists of the noting of the geographical co-ordinates of its position which can subsequently be found in the field through the use of a loran or GPS unit. The second technique involves the calculation of compass bearings of lines linking the position of the wreck with landmarks such as a lighthouse, a church tower or the point of a promontory. The angles between these bearings should be fairly open, ideally at 90°. The third technique

A

B

A - In order to localise wrecks, often situated at considerable depths and some distance from the shore, sonar equipment is often used. In this photo you can see the instrument which has located the wreck of the Togo, a ship lying in French waters.

*B - This image of the KT at Orosei was obtained via a EG & G 260 Side Scan Sonar with computer enhanced imaging. The scan was made by passing the sonar to one side of the wreck at a depth of around 20 metres. The dark area at the bottom is the so-called shadow, the area not read by the sonar.
Scan performed by Paolo Orrù*

is similar to the former, but rather than measuring bearings, it involves the identification of straight lines on the chart which, starting from the wreck, pass through two landmarks such as a lighthouse and a building, a tower and the peak of a mountain and so on. Having noted these data you can then proceed with the search for the wreck. None of the location techniques mentioned previously will ever allow you to locate the exact position of the wreck, but will provide you with a more or less precise area

in which it ought to lie. You should therefore have suitable equipment with which to continue the search at sea.
The most modern systems involve the use of special electronic instruments such as loran or GPS units which establish triangulations with terrestrial transmitters (loran) or satellites (GPS). The latter system would be far more precise than the former and less subject to interference if the satellite signals were not deliberately degraded for

military motives. Errors of reception are added to those due to the large scale of the nautical charts which leads to approximation in the marking of the wrecks.

The cumulative effect of these errors leads to a degree of precision which may vary from a matter of a couple of dozen metres to many hundreds. At times it is more effective to rely on the cheaper systems of compass bearings and alignments. With both methods you position yourself according to one of the lines plotted on the chart (a compass bearing or an alignment) and proceed along it until it intersects with the second. The principal instrument used during the fine-tooth combing of the search area is the echo-sounder. There are many different types on the market, most of them equipped with electronic digital displays which have now replaced the old mechanical systems. The best echo-sounder is still, however, the printing type which traces a precise profile of the sea-bed on a roll of thermal paper, providing a tangible record of the survey. The research begins with the identification of the point marked on the chart. You should immediately lower a shot line and marker buoy equipped with a locking reel which will let out just enough line to keep the buoy anchored vertically above the desired point. You can then perform a rapid survey of the area around the buoy with the echo-sounder, extending the perimeter of the search area in the case of negative results. You will often find that you have to mark a vast area with four more buoys and inspect it, following parallel sweeps that cover the area. You need patience and time, but the joy on finding a wreck by your own efforts repays the hours spent at sea sounding the bottom. With wrecks lying in shallow water you can also resort to the traditional search technique of dragging a wooden board attached to a rope behind a boat, using it as an elevator to measure the variations in depth. This is an efficient system at depths of up to 30-35 metres in clear water. The search concludes with the launching of a marker buoy which allows you to keep a trace on the position of the wreck in spite of waves and currents.

C

C - The bent propeller blades of the inner-right engine of the B-17 which was ditched in the waters off Calvi and now lies at 25 metres, suggest that the engine was still working when the plane hit the water.

D

D - Mediterranean waters are cold even in the summer, and you should use protective under garments as well as a good wet-suit, thick footwear and gloves. The diver portrayed here is exploring the KT at Orosei, a vessel which was sunk in 1943 by a torpedo launched by the submarine Safari.

E - A diver examining one of the tyres fitted to the undercarriage of the Canadair which crashed in the Gulf of Sagone on the 3rd of September, 1944. The use of good torch is always advisable when exploring wrecks.

E

Diving to a Mediterranean wreck is more demanding than a similar dive in tropical waters.

The wreck is usually lying at a greater depth, the water is much colder and, above all, visibility may well be limited due to the muddy nature of the sea-bed.

It would, therefore, be wise to sign up for a suitable wreck diving course, a speciality recognised by all the most modern teaching methods. There is a significant difference between diving to a coastal wreck and to one lying further off-shore on a more or less flat, muddy or sandy bottom.

In the first case the dive will be very similar to a normal dive entering the water from the shore or the shallows.

The only differences lie in the specific techniques used for exploring the wreck. The off-shore dive is a very different kettle of fish. It begins and ends with a long swim in open water with no visual reference points, and the diver is subjected to the effects of any currents in the area.

The type of dive is also different. In the first case it follows the classic multi-level pattern with an initial descent towards the greater depths followed by a gradual ascent which allows a partial desaturation of certain tissues.

In the case of a wreck lying on a flat bottom, the dive assumes a far more rectangular pattern given that virtually the whole dive is conducted at the maximum depth.

Each dive begins with an inspection of the equipment and careful programming.

There must be two demand valves, preferably independent and mounted on two separate first stage regulators.

This set-up allows any air leak due to a broken O-ring to be isolated by closing the relative valve.

The ideal demand valve fixture is the DIN type which prevents this type of accident and is also used by potholers. The demand valves must be overhauled regularly,

A

B

C

D

A - A group of divers approaching the Sagona, a freighter which sank after striking a mine on the 3rd of December, 1945 off the island of Porquerolles. You should never anchor directly above a wreck as it could cause damage.

B - The Romagna, an old tanker, sank in the Gulf of Cagliari on the 2nd of August, 1943 after striking a mine. Line lowered into the water makes descending to a wreck easier.

have a perfectly sound harness arranged in such a way as not to snag on the wreck structures.

Your buoyancy compensator (BC) should be of a reasonable size to compensate for the compression of your wet-suit at greater depths and to provide a good degree of buoyancy in case of emergencies. A good knife, not long but sharp,

is indispensable. It will be used to cut through the tangles of fishing lines, nets and cords which conceal many wrecks. It would be a good idea to have a spare knife to be kept in the pocket of the BC should you drop or lose the first one. A good torch or flashlight is necessary for exploring the darker areas, and should you decide to penetrate the interior of the wreck you will also need a spare lamp. Again for exploration of the more inaccessible sections, in certain cases you will need an Arianne's thread wound onto a spool which you let out as you proceed. Lastly, it should not be forgotten that beyond a certain depth the waters of the Mediterranean are cold even in summer, with temperatures varying between 15° and 18°. Thermal insulation should thus be adequate, and as well as a good wet-suit you should wear a jerkin below your suit and thick footwear and gloves. We are now going to take a look at the techniques used during the descent on an off-shore wreck lying on a muddy bottom at a good depth. This represents the most difficult and demanding type of dive. You should never anchor directly over the wreck, given that the anchor itself would damage and get lodged in the wreck. There are two alternatives: either the cover boat follows your air bubbles without dropping anchor, or the anchor can be dropped to one side of the wreck. In both cases the descent should be made by following a shot line attached to a marker buoy lowered over the centre of the wreck. It is incredible how psychologically useful it can be to have a guideline to follow. When diving off-shore you should always be aware of the possibility of currents. These currents can be identified by studying the inclination of the buoy, you should enter the water only moments before beginning the actual dive, preferably slightly upstream of the buoy.

The descent should be rapid but not so fast as to risk depth drunkenness. When you begin to see the wreck you should slow up, inflating the BC so that you achieve neutral buoyancy before touching the structure. It is better to begin the exploration by finning over the wreck in open water so as to get a good idea of its shape. You should swim down to the wreck when this examination is complete, trying to avoid stirring up the sediment and making good use of your BC. You should not forget that the ascent must take place along the same

E

F

shot line as the descent and that each exploratory dive comprises a descent and a subsequent ascent. The air supply should be apportioned 1/3 for the outward trip, 1/3 for the return and 1/3 for the ascent, any decompression stops and an emergency supply. In any case a spare air supply should be lowered to a suitable depth below the boat as a precautionary measure.

G

C - The torch allows you to admire the colouring of the organisms which encrust the Rubis.

D - To make the most of a dive to a wreck, you should swim over it in open water so as to gain a clear idea of the layout.

E - A photographer illuminates a section of the Liban, the liner which sank off Marseilles on the 7th of June, 1903.

F - Entering wrecks is always fairly risky, although the appeal of visiting the interior of a sunken ship is undeniable. In this photo a diver has ventured inside the Chauen, a Moroccan freighter which sank off the island of Le Planier on the 21st of February, 1970.

G - Diving to wrecks like the Genova, a steamship which sank off Punta Portofino on the 27th of July, 1917, largely shrouded with nets, requires great care.

FAUNA

Each and every wreck represents a boon not only for divers, but also for the many forms of life which are presented with a vast and favourable new complex to colonise in an environment in which the housing shortage is always dramatic.
Among the first sessile organisms to stake a claim to the new structures are algae, especially at depths of up to a few metres where photosynthesis is still possible thanks to the strong sunlight.
In just a few weeks bryozoa, annelids and molluscs also start to colonise the wreck and develop quite rapidly.
The areas most densely populated are those exposed to currents where the coelenterates can feed on the nutrients brought by the mass of moving water.
From depths of just a few metres the surfaces of the wreck will be covered with yellow and white sea fans *(Eunicella cavolinii* and *singularis)*, whilst in deeper waters the red *Paramuricea clavata* also appears. Some organisms avoid light and prefer protected sites such as the ceilings of cabins or the lower side of the hull. In these areas you find madrepores such as the yellow "buttons" of *Leptopsammia pruvoti* and formations of *Cladocora caespitosa*.
The innermost cabins where the water is virtually still are less popular, and even after many years they are colonised only by spiral tube-worms and a few bryozoa and maintain a very "clean" appearance. This is not true where there is a good flow of water as in this case even red coral may be found growing on the plating. There will also be significant colonies of sponges, especially the encrusting *Spirastrella cuctatrix* and *Phorbas tenacior* and the beautiful *Aplysina aerophoba* which is capable of covering large areas with yellow clusters.

Lastly, mention should also be made of the presence on certain wrecks of one of the most attractive Mediterranean organisms, a corallimorpharia *(Corynactis viridis)*, which may assume various colourings ranging from brown to pink by way of green and yellow, with a particular fuchsia tone which is truly explosive in the darkness of the depths.
Fissures and other tight spaces are ideal for crustaceans, lobsters, galatheidea and various species of prawns. These animals are easily found at night when they hunt. As for the fish, the masters of the wrecks are the conger eels which may reach enormous dimensions and which choose to inhabit the most inaccessible areas such as tubes and boilers or between the hull and the sea-bed. Also common are schools of Anthias, fork beards, scorpionfish and sea breams, especially sharp snout sea breams *(Diplodus puntazzo)* which swim in open water above the wrecks.

A

B

C

A - Scorpionfish are a common sight when diving to wrecks.

B - Among the fish which have chosen to take up residence in wrecks are conger eels (Conger conger). The examples shown here inhabit the wreck of the Tantine, a rather mysterious vessel whose history is completely unknown.

C - It is fairly difficult to take good photographs of large wrecks like the Amerique, a steamship which sank early this century close to

Torre Faro, at the extreme North of the Sicilian coast of the Strait of Messina. You should use very wide-angle lenses.

PHOTOGRAPHY AND VIDEO

D - A photographer
studying the plates
encrusted with
organisms and
adorned with
gorgonians of the
stern section of
the Mohawk Deer.
The Mediterranean
waters contain a
lot of suspended
matter which
makes sharp
images difficult
to obtain.

E - Photographs are
the only souvenirs
to be taken to the
surface by divers
after the exploration
of a wreck. Above
right a fully
equipped diver
seeks the best way
to "immortalize" one
of the vehicles
characteristic of the
wreck of the Nasim II.
It is of great
importance
underwater to
check carefully the
intensity of light.
Correct illumination
is essential for good
photographs and
the use of a flash,
at all depths, is
often not
recommended
for the risk of
highlighting
particles in
suspension.

Photographing Mediterranean wrecks is really very difficult, especially if you are trying to capture the sheer size of a large wreck rather than a particular detail. In either case you should use very wide-angle lenses, the only type which allows you to photograph a large portion of the wreck from a reasonable distance.

The water is in fact rich in suspended matter and the quality and sharpness of the image is inversely proportional to distance which separates the camera from the subject. If the wreck is lying in shallow water where the natural light is still strong the problems can be overcome.

In this case all you need to do is switch off the flash which would only illuminate the suspended particles and keep the camera still while you take the photograph. You will often be suspended in open water, perfectly balanced by the BC.

At greater depths however it becomes very difficult, if not impossible, to render the dimensions of a large vessel. Again, flash units should not be used except for lighting the foreground, with the light source being kept very off-set.

Exposure times will be so long that there will be a risk of blurred images. You may fall back on faster films, but the results will inevitably be grainy, making the image even more fuzzy and less well defined.

A flash unit, or better still two units when using ultra-wide-angle lenses, can be used for close-up shots. You should never shoot where another diver has already passed as the image would be ruined by the suspended matter, and you should always remember to keep the lighting units off-set and as far away from the camera as possible.

For shots taken inside the wreck you need a pilot lamp on the flash unit, and a light by which

to read shutter speed, aperture and distance scales.

The internal walls will help to reflect part of the light and you will be able to illuminate large spaces. You will have to work quickly, however, before your bubbles start bringing down a veritable rain of particles. Similar problems have to be overcome with video shooting. Again you need very wide-angle lenses; the standard zoom lenses mounted on cameras are rarely

sufficiently wide. You have to utilize add-on wide-angle lenses. Occasionally these are provided by the manufacturer.

The best method of lighting for video is to give a light source to your subject so as to shorten the distance the light has to travel. Even with lamps mounted on the camera casing, moving images are much more forgiving of a lack of sharpness caused by suspended matter than a still photograph.

SAN DOMENICO
by Kurt Amsler

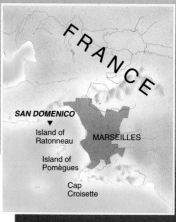

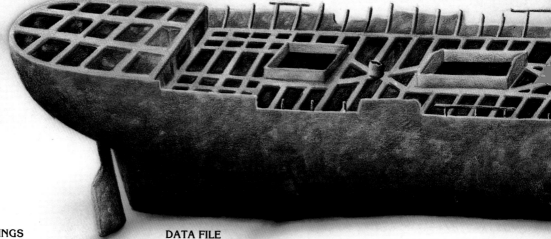

RATINGS

Location difficulty: minimum.
Visibility: quite good.
Currents: scarce.
Diving difficulty: minimum.
Lines or nets: many.
Historical interest: high.
Photographic interest: high.
Biological interest: average.

DATA FILE

Type of wreck: three master
    sailing ship.
Nationality: Italian.
Date of construction: 1893.
Tonnage: 1,119 tonnes.
Date of sinking: 6.16.1897.
Cause of sinking: excessive rolling
    of the ship.
Geographical co-ordinates:
    43°18,36'8" N, 5°20'48,9" O.
Localisation: northern Marseilles Bay.
Distance from the shore: 800 metres.
Minimum depth: 26 metres.
Maximum depth: 33 metres.

THE SAN DOMENICO

A - At 70 metres long, the San Domenico is one of the largest Mediterranean wrecks. Even though the vessel has been reduced to little more than an empty shell, diving to this wreck is still spectacular, thanks above all to the extraordinary clarity of the water.

B - Many of the ship's features have disappeared due to the destructive action of the water in which she has been lying for almost a century.

C - The prow of the San Domenico, which is lying upright on the sea-bed, is pointing towards the entrance to the port of Marseilles.

Marseilles, the 16th of June, 1897: the three-master *San Domenico*, a classic engineless sailing ship typical of the era, was anchored in the old port.

Even though the she was only four years old, she already found herself in dock requiring maintenance work, and was due to move on to the nearby Estanque yard in order for all the necessary repairs to be made. As the distance to be covered was minimal it was not thought necessary to set the sails and the *San Domenico* was towed as far as the Vieux Port basin by the tug Marsellaise.

On that day the mistral was blowing down from the Rodano valley at Force 10. The *San Domenico* was manned only by Captain Domenico Gavagnin and a few sailors.

The sea was choppy and it was thus particularly difficult to unfurl the sails; suddenly, even though it was well built and extremely stable in normal conditions, the ship began to roll.

The problem can be put down to the lack of 100 tonnes of ballast which was usually located in the keel. Captain Gavagnin immediately realised the reason for his ship's strange behaviour: a serious error in the organization of the transfer had been committed. There was no time to pass judgement, however, and Gavagnin was powerless as he had no means of manoeuvring. The *San Domenico* began to wallow, oscillating in such a way as to appear to be on the point of capsizing from one moment to the next, and each time she rolled she took on huge quantities of water. The lapse of time between one oscillation and the next increased dramatically and the ship was upright ever more rarely, and for increasingly brief periods. Suddenly the whole port side of the ship was in the water and she sank rapidly.

The three-master's crew and that of the tug were completely unprepared for such an event. The captain of the tug was even afraid that his ship, having got caught up in the rigging, would

be dragged down with the *San Domenico*. In those brief moments dominated by general panic, some sailors succeeded in boarding the tug whilst others jumped into the water. Unfortunately, despite the attempts to rescue them, three men drowned.

In spite of the fact that the *San Domenico* sank just half a mile off the coast in relatively shallow water, no attempts were made to salvage her. The long bowsprit and the masts which were no more than three metres from the

surface, were cut so as to ensure that they did not interfere with the other shipping in the area.

Diving to the wreck

The wreck of the *San Domenico* is to be found in the Northern roadstead of Marseilles at an ideal depth of 33 metres.

The prow of the ship is still facing in the direction of the port which she was unfortunately never to reach. The *San Domenico* is lying on a sandy sea-bed with a slight list to starboard. At this point, just half a mile from the basin, the currents are hardly ever strong and the whole area is sheltered from the wind. The ship is 70 metres long and varies from 6 to 8 metres in height. Unfortunately, as mentioned above, the masts and bowsprit are no longer in place, but nevertheless the dive is truly unforgettable, thanks in part to the clarity of the water which usually aids exploration of the wreck. Visibility within the Marseilles basin is by no means good, and yet just outside the water is exceptionally clear, and the shape of the *San Domenico* can be made out clearly from above. As you swim closer you begin to be able to see the characteristic features of the wreck such as the broad stern with its broken rudder to the starboard side. It is no good looking for the ship's propeller, given that ships of this era used the wind as their only motive power! The hull has been completely covered with bivalves and when you illuminate it with your torch it seems to be a delicate orange carpet.

The wooden planking of the deck are almost all rotten, ruined by the exposure to water and the continual motion of the sea. Passing through the ribs, you can enter the hull, but it should be pointed out that very little remains of the supports of the three masts which were once to be found here. During your exploration of the wreck it is worth pausing to look at the breathtaking panorama offered by the forward section: enormous nets hang between the beams and, together with the rays of sunlight filtering down from the surface, create a stunning composition.

You will not fail to meet up with the usual inhabitants of the Mediterranean wrecks: a number of large eels, the inevitable scorpionfish, friendly morays and schools of sardines.

Innumerable yellow snails up to 10 centimeters long are a feature of this wreck.

Similar to an enormous funeral veil, a vast net hangs along the starboard side of the ship.

It is thus preferable to dive some way from the vessel, favouring the side towards the open sea. This also allows you to enjoy the spectacle of the net draped around the stern.

It really is a pity that the bowsprit is no longer in place; this element

D

E

F

D - The wooden planking which once covered the decks has almost all rotted away, exposing the underlying metal ribs and thus creating a rather surreal effect.

E - The forward section of the San Domenico *is wrapped in a trawl-net which got caught up on the wreck and was abandoned. Even though the ship has been reduced to a mass of sediment encrusted scrap metal, she is still a very evocative sight.*

F - Through the various apertures which have opened up in the deck you can - carefully - make your way into the interior of the great sailing ship. Here you will find all the usual wreck inhabitants from snails to moray eels.

is now to be found a short distance form the prow, half buried in the sand.

The dive to the *San Domenico* is fairly simple: thanks to relatively shallow waters in which she is lying you have plenty of time in which to explore the whole of the wreck.

However, it would be as well to remember that you are diving in heavily trafficked waters and you should both dive from and emerge at your cover boat.

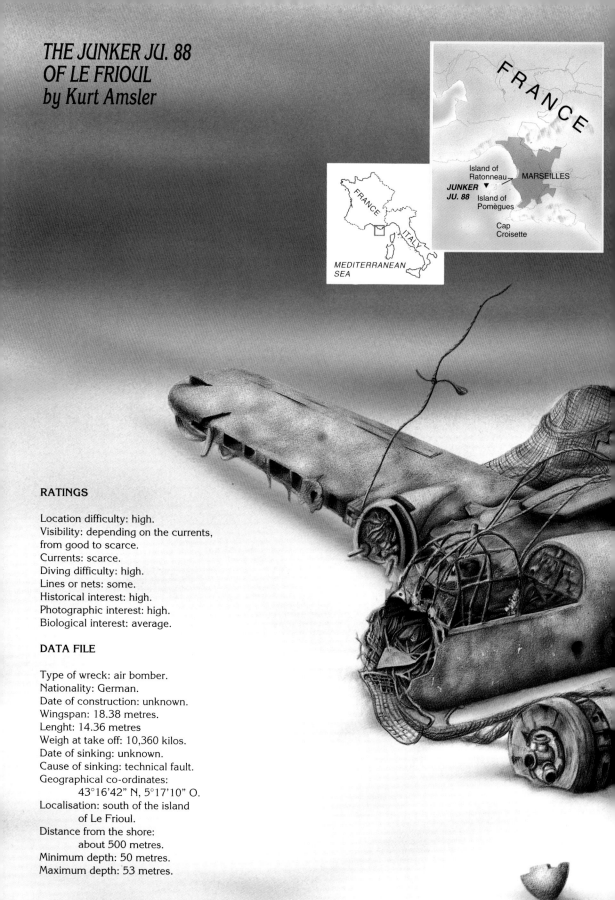

THE JUNKER JU. 88
OF LE FRIOUL
by Kurt Amsler

RATINGS

Location difficulty: high.
Visibility: depending on the currents,
from good to scarce.
Currents: scarce.
Diving difficulty: high.
Lines or nets: some.
Historical interest: high.
Photographic interest: high.
Biological interest: average.

DATA FILE

Type of wreck: air bomber.
Nationality: German.
Date of construction: unknown.
Wingspan: 18.38 metres.
Lenght: 14.36 metres
Weigh at take off: 10,360 kilos.
Date of sinking: unknown.
Cause of sinking: technical fault.
Geographical co-ordinates:
        43°16'42" N, 5°17'10" O.
Localisation: south of the island
        of Le Frioul.
Distance from the shore:
        about 500 metres.
Minimum depth: 50 metres.
Maximum depth: 53 metres.

FRANCE

FRANCE
ITALY
MEDITERRANEAN
SEA

Island of
Ratonneau
MARSEILLES
JUNKER ▼
JU. 88
Island of
Pomègues
Cap
Croisette

50 m

53 m

N

THE JUNKER JU. 88

Nothing is known for certain about how this German bomber came to be lying at the bottom of the sea. It is said that she was based at Istre, the Luftwaffe airfield close to Avignon, and it is presumed that a technical fault forced the pilot to ditch his plane.

This theory is plausible in that the aircraft is lying not far from the island of Le Frioul to which the aircrew were able to swim. Unfortunately, however, we know that not all the occupants of the plane escaped from the accident

unharmed, as human bones were found in the cockpit. There is an eye witness, a gendarme serving on the island, who claims to have seen an aircraft go down in 1944 more or less in the area in which "our" wreck is to be found. However, the fact that under the pilot's seat of the *Junker Ju. 88* was found a flare with a still legible "use-by" date of May, 1943, does not fit with this thesis: if we are to rely on the usual precision of the Luftwaffe, the *Junker Ju. 88* must have been lost earlier.

As parts of the aircraft are covered with a heavy net of the type used for deep water fishing,

it may well be that a trawler picked up the wreck in her nets and dragged it to shallower waters before cutting it free, perhaps to save the net.

Around 16,000 examples of the *Junker Ju. 88* were built between 1939 and 1945.

Considered to be the backbone of the Luftwaffe, it was employed in many roles, and proved to be the Germans' most versatile aircraft. As well as being an effective bomber it could also be used for reconnaissance and as a nightfighter.

The wreck was discovered by Luc Vanrell in 1989, and the Marseilles diver continues to visit the aircraft in the hope of finding

A - This archive photograph portrays the front machine-gun of a Junker Ju. 88, mounted on the right-hand side of the cockpit. This weapon with a fairly restricted filed of fire was only fitted to certain production batches.

B - The Junker Ju. 88 was probably the best German bomber of the Second World War, and undoubtedly the model produced in the greatest numbers: numerous different versions for a total 16,000 examples came off the assembly lines between 1939 and 1945.

an object or a document that might help him to reveal her secrets.

Diving to the wreck

The wreck of this twin-engined aircraft is lying approximately a kilometre and a half from the island of Le Frioul at a depth of around 53 metres. She is resting on sand as neatly as if she had been parked in a hanger; the tail is bent at an angle of 45°, but all the other structural elements of the plane are completely intact. The bomber is 14.5 metres long and has a wingspan of a little under 20 metres. The glazed nose is buckled, probably as a result of the impact with the sea. Parts of the *Junker Ju. 88*, the tail and the left-hand wing, are wrapped in a wide-mesh net. When you begin your dive to this aircraft and are descending through the blue waters, you should pause at a depth of around ten metres. From this point you will be able to admire the wreck in its entirety. As the bomber is small, in contrast with other deep wrecks you will have time to examine everything. Among the most interesting elements are the engines, which although they lack their propellers, really are impressive. The *Junker Ju. 88*'s were generally equipped with Jumo 211 B, 1200 hp engines, or 213 E units developing 1725 hp.

C

D

C - A diver hovering over the left-hand wing of the bomber; in foreground you can see the point at which the fuselage was truncated.

D - The leading edges of both wings suffered considerable damage when the plane hit the waves: parts of the complex structure of ribs and dural longerons can thus be seen.

E - Like most bombers of the era, the Junker Ju. 88 had a fully glazed nose which housed the bomb aimer, the crew member responsible for releasing the bombs. This part of the aircraft is seriously damaged.

E

A - The framework of the cockpit over has been preserved relatively intact; in the centre you can still see the point where, during some missions, the forward machine-gun was housed.

B - One of the large wheels and tyres of the undercarriage can still be seen trapped below one of the wings.

C - The pilot and co-pilot's seats are still mounted one beside the other in the cockpit, surrounded by much of the instrumentation.

Unfortunately we have not been able to identify which engines were fitted to "our" aircraft. If you brush away the sand from the left-hand wing around a third of its length from the tip, you will see the German markings: a black and white cross. The aircraft is lying on a sandy sea-bed in a fairly isolated spot and it can thus be fairly described as an underwater oasis. Many fish have set up home in the wreck and a number of lobsters can be seen below the wings. All around the plane swim numbers of graceful scorpionfish, a common fish around most wrecks, whilst spectacular yellow encrusting spiral tube-worms have colonised the tail. A number of points have to be made about the planning of this dive and the safety of those involved. The *Ju. 88* is to be found at a depth of 53 metres and the exploration of the wreck requires considerable experience of deep diving as well as suitable equipment. For a complete and satisfactory dive it is very important to localize the wreck precisely so as to anchor your cover boat no more than a few metres to one side: swimming any distance at such depths is tiring and also time consuming. Lastly, you should bear in mind that in the case of heavy rain, strong winds or currents from the West (the Rodano brings down considerable quantities of sediment), visibility is considerably reduced and the wreck can only be seen from a few metres away.

D - A diver closely examining the enormous spinner of the left-hand engine's propeller: clearly the three metal blades of which you can see the housings, were lost during the violent crash, when the plane hit the waves

E - The Junker Ju. 88 was powered by two Jumo engines, the same units that were fitted to the famous Stuka dive-bombers; during the war the original 1,200 hp type 211 B's were replaced with 1,725 hp type 213 E's.

F - A fine-mesh fishing net is wrapped around the tail-plane which is lying on the right-hand wing.

G - You can still clearly see the Nazi markings on one wing tip, a black cross bordered in white. Similar markings appeared on the undersides of the wings and either side of the fuselage.

LIBAN
by Kurt Amsler

RATINGS

Location difficulty: minimum.
Visibility: quite good.
Currents: none.
Diving difficulty: minimum.
Lines or nets: none.
Historical interest: high.
Photographic interest: high.
Biological interest: high.

DATA FILE

Type of wreck: passenger ship.
Nationality: French.
Date of construction: 1882.
Tonnage: 2,308 tonnes.
Date of sinking: 6.7.1903.
Cause of sinking: collision with
        steamship *Insulaire*.
Geographical co-ordinates:
        43°12'26" N, 5°20'14" O.
Localisation: in front of the island
        of Les Farillons.
Distance from the shore:
        about 20 metres.
Minimum depth: 30 metres.
Maximum depth: 36 metres.

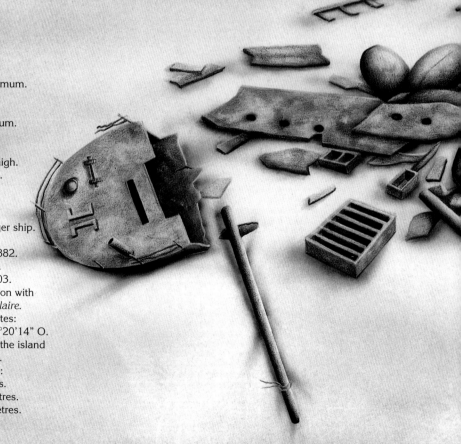

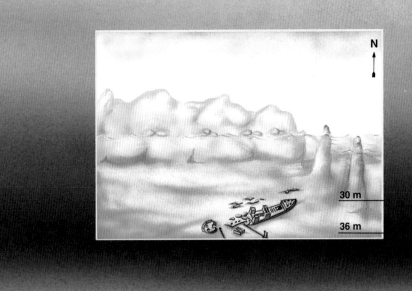
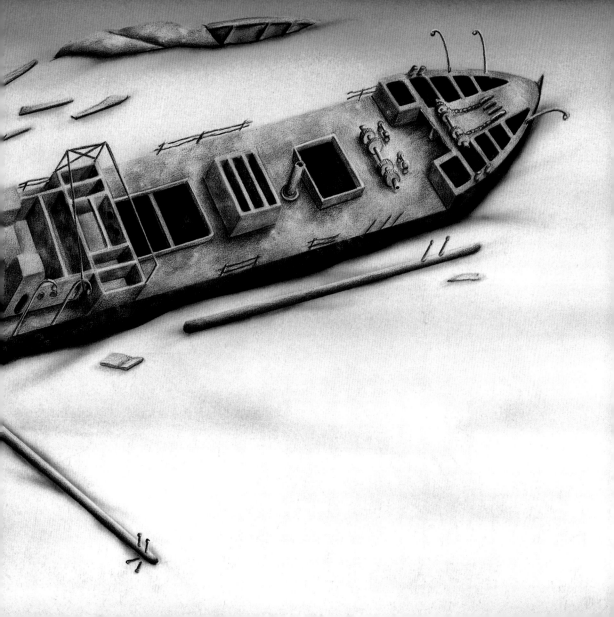

30 m

36 m

N

THE LIBAN

The tragic loss of the passenger ship *Liban* led to the deaths of almost 200 people, and it is considered to be the greatest catastrophe to have occurred in the waters of the French port of Marseilles. It really is difficult to imagine quite how a disaster of this magnitude could have occurred that weekend, on Sunday, the 3rd of June, 1903. It is not known whether it was a storm or poor visibility, or perhaps even a technical fault, which caused the *Liban* with its full complement of passengers to collide with the steamship the *Insulaire*. Both vessels had been observed off the island of Tiboulen de Mairé at which time visibility was down to about 100 metres. The captains of the two ships intended to pass by and ordered a turn to starboard. This was generally a straightforward manoeuvre in open seas, and the *Liban* duly changed course. The *Insulaire* on the other hand was obstructed by the nearby island of Mairé, and to avoid striking the rocks the captain ordered a turn hard to port so as to cancel out his original order. Suddenly the prow of the *Insulaire* struck the *Liban*, gashing her port flank and penetrating deep inside the ship. This took place at 12.30. Aboard the *Liban*, Captain Lacotte gave desperate orders to try to free his ship from the prow of the *Insulaire* and when he eventually succeeded he immediately realised the extent of the damage.
Well aware of the gravity of the situation, he decided to take his vessel as close in to the shore of the island of Mairé as possible. Unfortunately the almost vertical rock walls prevented the passengers from landing.
The captain thus decided to head full steam towards another safe "berth", the rocks of Les Farillons. Here, between two outcrops rising from the sea, he intended to save his ship by running her aground. As soon as he began to relax, thinking that he had succeeded,

LA CATASTROPHE DU « LIBAN »
Le sauvetage des passagers

the unforeseeable happened: just 20 metres from the rocks the stern of the *Liban* began to rise slowly above the surface of the sea.
As her propeller churned the air, the ship began to vibrate dramatically as she wallowed helplessly immobile. At that point the men aboard the ship realised that she was sinking bow first, initially very slowly but then increasingly quickly. The end was so rapid and unexpected that the crew did not even have time to lower the lifeboats. The scene must have been truly horrific: many

A - The wrecking of the Liban, *documented in this original illustration, was one of the most serious marine catastrophes ever to happen in French waters: over two hundred crew members and passengers perished.*

B - In this photograph, taken shortly after the disaster, the prow of the Insulaire *appears visibly damaged by the fatal impact against the* Liban.

C - The Liban *sank in just a few minutes, to the accompaniment of general chaos amidst which the crew did not even have time to lower the boast. Even though numerous vessels responded to the distress calls, the rescue operations were uncoordinated and, as this illustration of the era shows, the incident developed into an veritable tragedy.*

D - The spectral wreck of the large steam-ship is lying on sand at a depth varying between 30 and 36 metres. In this shot you can see a number of lifeboat derricks.

people panicked, jumped into the sea and drowned either because they could not swim or because they were obstructed by their heavy, wet clothes. Others made vain attempts to take refuge by climbing the masts or the highest parts of the superstructure, but as the ship inclined ever more steeply they fell either to the decks or directly into the sea. The general panic was exacerbated the screams of the passengers and the crewmen and the frantic whistling of the ship's valves echoing around the rocks. The situation was truly chaotic. Numerous ships responded to Mayday signal and soon congregated in the area; they quickly lowered their boats, but a systematic rescue operation was impossible due to the ungovernable confusion. A great explosion suddenly ripped the air: the ship's boiler had burst, and with a deafening crack and accompanied by scalding jets of steam, the vessel split in two. When a measure of calm returned to the raging surface of the sea, the *Liban* had disappeared, inexorably swallowed up by the waves. The passengers, particularly those who had taken refuge on the canvas-covered quarterdeck were dragged down with the ship. It has never been possible to establish the precise number of the victims: the shipping company spoke of 90 deaths, whilst the newspapers describing the sinking of the *Liban* wrote that at least 180 people had lost their lives. This uncertainty is due to the fact that the ship had only just set sail and not all the

passengers had had time to complete the registration formalities. Moreover, for some time there was a rather persistent rumour to the effect that a number of chained prisoners on their way to the labour camps on Corsica had been trapped below decks. Numerous legal proceedings were taken up with the aim of revealing the precise sequence of events which led up to the tragic accident; three years later the *Insulair*

captain was condemned for having given that fatal counter-order, and for having returned to port with no thought for the possible consequences and the eventual destiny of the *Liban*. The ship was abandoned in its "tomb", on the Eastern side of the island of Mairé, and there were never any attempts to salvage her. On the other hand, the *Insulair* crossed the Atlantic after the necessary repairs had been made to her prow.

E - Numerous furnishing and decorative elements have been recovered from the Liban over the years, including this female statue and pedestal which probably decorated one of the vessel's saloons.

F - All the objects recovered from the interior of the wreck were heavily encrusted because of their stay at the bottom of the sea: the ship has been lying on the sea-bed off Marseilles since the 7th of June, 1903.

G - Even though it is heavily encrusted, this capstan is still recognisable.

Diving to the wreck

The area in which the wreck of the *Liban* is to be found, close the rocks of Les Farillons, is protected from the winds from the North, but completely exposed to the waves raised by those from the South and the East. The ship is around 90 metres long and is lying at a depth varying from 30 metres (at the prow) to 36 metres (the stern). You are advised to begin your dive at the stern, the deepest point.
This section of the ship, like much of the keel, is listing at 45° to the sea-bed.
It really is worthwhile pausing to examine details of this imposing steamship such as the lines of the quarterdeck and the steering gear. If you swim over the bulwark and down to the rudder you can see the bronze propeller, partly buried in the sand.

A - The wreck is completely covered with lush colonies of gorgonians and madrepores, some of which are so well developed as to make certain structural elements of the ship unrecognisable.

B - The deck, the superstructure, the companionways and the cabins are largely intact. Exploring these areas is extremely exciting even for the most experienced divers.

C - A diver approaches a porthole and shines his torch into one of the passenger cabins. The Liban *was a fairly luxurious vessel and sailed between Marseilles and Corsica.*

Here, in the shadowed area, the hull is completely covered with myriad marvellous sea-fans and, with the aid of your torch, you will be able to admire their typical dark red colouring.
You then begin ascending towards the prow; after having the examined the stern which is still in good condition, you swim over an expanse of scrap metal before reaching the enormous boiler which presents clear evidence of the explosion. Having seen the devastating effects of the blast, it is easy to understand why the ship sank so rapidly.
The highest parts of the superstructure provide excellent shelter from the currents, as well as offering numerous areas of interest. In spite of its desolation, the *Liban* is animated by the extraordinary forms of life to be found in the Mediterranean.
For example, above the saloon, once one of the ship's glories, you may well meet a dense school of damselfish comprising thousands of examples.
There are also numerous, heavily populated schools of snappers which patrol the decks.
Hidden among the distorted metalwork, you may find large congers which, illuminated by your torch, will glare at you with their round black eyes.
The wealth of underwater life to be found on the *Liban* provides continual surprises and sensations even for expert divers.
While the deeper parts of the wreck are completely covered with lush colonies of sea-fans, the higher sections such as the deck, the metal structures and the gangways are no less fertile. Here, in fact, yellow polyps of solitary corals dominates the scene. At this point of the dive the deck is almost level, and the imposing anchor winch marks the prow. From here you have a panoramic view of much of the wreck: from the port bulwark, with its small derricks, to the raised prow and one of the main masts which, together with many other items of wreckage is lying on the sand to the starboard side.

D

E

F

D - A diver illuminating a large wheel, still perfectly recognisable amidst the wreckage of the engine-room.

E - The magnificent prow of the Liban *is lying with a slight list to one side; this photograph clearly shows the stem and, on the port side, two derricks.*

F - Given that the wreck is lying in fairly shallow waters, this exploration can be made by divers of all levels of experience. However, only experts should venture inside the wreck.

As far as diving safety is concerned, you will not have to descend to any great depths and so divers of all degrees of experience will be able to explore the *Liban* easily.
You should carry at least 3,000 litres of air and, as mentioned earlier, begin your dive at the deepest point, that is to say the stern of the ship, and then ascend towards the prow where you will be able to pause for longer.
You should of course equip yourself with a good torch so that you can illuminate the countless magnificent sea-fans, and discover the fish tucked away in their dens.

THE MESSERSCHMITT BF. 109 OF LE PLANIER
by Kurt Amsler

RATINGS

Location difficulty: minimum.
Visibility: from good to very good.
Currents: scarce.
Diving difficulty: from average to high.
Lines or nets: none.
Historical interest: high.
Photographic interest: high.
Biological interest: average.

DATA FILE

Type of wreck: air fighter.
Nationality: German.
Date of construction: unknown.
Wingspan: 9.86 metres.
Lenght: 8.84 metres.
Weight at take off: 3.386 kilos.
Date of crash: 3.7.1944.
Cause of crash: engine failure.
Geographical co-ordinates:
      43°12'7" N, 5°13'85" O.
Localisation: north of the island
      of Le Planier.
Distance from the shore:
      about 100 metres.
Minimum depth: 44 metres.
Maximum depth: 45 metres.

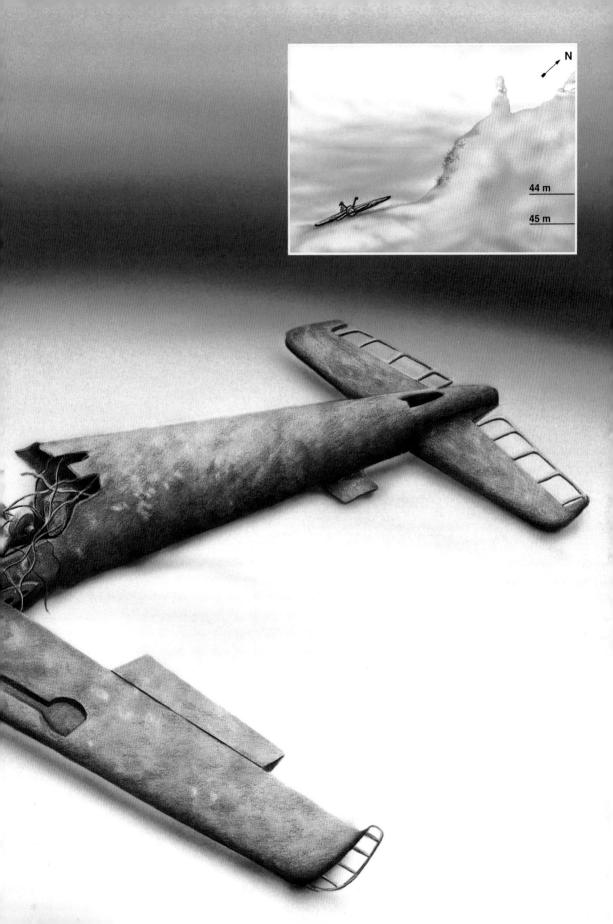

THE MESSERSCHMITT BF. 109

On the 7th of March, 1944 the air raid warning sounded over the Luftwaffe base close to Avignon. Two American *B-17* bombers, escorted by two Lightning fighters, were closing in on the port of Marseilles. Two *Messerschmitt Bf. 109*'s, the formidable German fighters, were immediately despatched to intercept the enemy aircraft. One of the German pilots was Captain Hans Fahrenberger - a name uncovered after years of careful research by the French wreck specialist J. P. Joncheray - and the mission very nearly cost him his life: it was something of a miracle that he survived.

The enemy bombers were soon sighted by the two German pilots who showed no hesitation in pressing home their attack. They employed the classic fighter pilot's tactic of coming out of the glare of the sun so that the bomber crews would be caught unawares by the small, fast German fighters. Captain Fahrenberger dived steeply, firing at the *B-17*'s with the 30 mm cannon mounted in the hub of his plane's propeller. However, perhaps due to the strong gusts of wind buffeting the *Messerschmitt* he missed the target. The Captain thus prepared to launch a second attack and forced his plane into a near vertical climb.

Unfortunately for him his engine choose that moment to cut out

A, B - These photos show two Messerschmitt Bf. 109's in action; the formidable German fighters were noted above all for their agility and fire-power.

A

B

suddenly. His position could have been worse, however, as he had plenty of height to try to glide to a safe landing and the American Lightnings were not following him; they may have noticed the smoke from his damaged engine and decided to leave him to his fate. His considerable flying skills and experience allowed the captain to nurse his plane as far as the small lighthouse island of Le Planier. He ditched the *Messerschmitt* just 100 metres from the rocks on a sea lashed by the gusting wind.

As Captain Fahrenberger recalls "the water sprayed everywhere, one of the propeller blades snapped like a matchstick and the metal skin of the aircraft creased and deformed as if they were made of cardboard.
The *Messerschmitt* sank like a stone in just five or six seconds. I don't know how, but I succeeded in opening the canopy and found myself in an air bubble which immediately carried me upwards. I would have drowned but for my parachute which helped me to reach the surface.
The pilot reached the safety of the island of Le Planier where, after a day's wait, he was spotted by a German patrol boat which

C - Today, Captain Hans Fahrenberger can afford to smile at the memory of the terrible incident from which he emerged unscathed in the March of 1944.

D - The Messerschmitt *Bf. 109 was ditched just 100 metres off the small island of Le Planier, dominated by its imposing lighthouse.*

E, F -The up-turned undercarriage of the Messerschmitt *Bf. 109 wreck bears testimony to the violence and drama with which the plane crashed into the sea.*

took him on board. The downed fighter was a single-engined machine baptised with the name of its designer the engineer Willy Messerschmitt.
It was equipped with a remarkable 2,000 hp engine providing it with a maximum speed of 727 kph. It was particularly noted and feared for its diving attacks from high altitudes.

Diving to the wreck

The wreck of the *Messerschmitt* can be found about 100 metres off the island of Le Planier at a depth of 45 metres. The aircraft is just 8.74 metres long with a wingspan of 9.86 metres.
The waters surrounding the island are fairly clear and the wreck can be seen from some distance. When conditions of visibility are good the dive can be made from the island itself.
The *MesserschmittBf. 109* is lying upside down with the undercarriage uppermost.
One propeller blade is buried in the sand, whilst the others are broken. The rudder and tail planes are distorted due to unsuccessful attempts by divers to lift the wreck to discover what secrets were hidden in the aircraft's cockpit. The wreck is lying on a broad expanse of sand and is a veritable aquatic oasis. The barrel of the 30 mm cannon in the propeller spinner houses a number of

A - A diver carefully examining the plane's engine, today covered with innumerable, multi-coloured encrustations.

B - Even after so many years on the sea-bed, one of the plane's propeller blades and the muzzle of the 30 mm cannon located in the spinner can be clearly seen.

C - The metal skin of the fuselage was also irreparably damaged and distorted when the plane hit the waves.

congers, whilst large annelids encrust the wings and undercarriage. If you illuminate the plane with your torch prepare to be astonished by the extraordinary colouring of the sponges which cover the interior. As the wreck is relatively small you must move carefully.

Any disturbance of the sand will reduce visibility immediately. Those of you who want to take photographs must be especially careful in this respect.

Lastly, if you swim to the South, towards the island, after having explored the wreck of the *Messerschmitt* you will emerge close to a rock wall extraordinarily rich in wonderful sea fans.

D

E

D - The Messerschmitt *is not only a submerged and forgotten memorial to the tragedies of the Second World War; it is also home to innumerable forms of life such as this graceful urchin hanging from a completely encrusted tube.*

E - The dazzling colours of the infinite forms of life which have colonised the aircraft form a backdrop to a delicate spiral tube-worms.

F

F - Scorpionfish are also among the inhabitants of the wreck; an example can be seen "posing" on the aircraft in this photograph.

CHAUEN
by Kurt Amsler

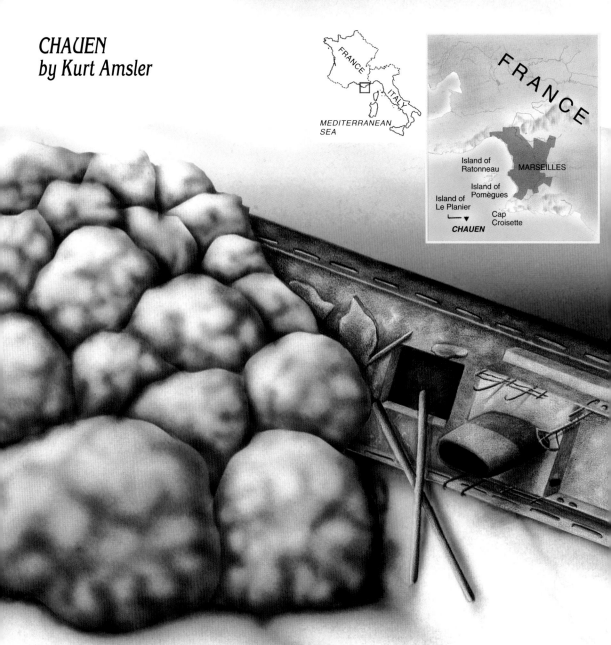

FRANCE
ITALY
MEDITERRANEAN
SEA

FRANCE

Island of
Ratonneau   MARSEILLES

Island of
Pomègues
Island of
Le Planier
Cap
Croisette
CHAUEN

RATINGS

Location difficulty: minimum.
Visibility: from good to very good.
Currents: scarce.
Diving difficulty: minimum.
Lines or nets: cables inside the wreck.
Historical interest: low.
Photographic interest: high.
Biological interest: average.

DATA FILE

Type of wreck: merchant ship.
Nationality: Moroccan.
Date of construction: 1960.
Tonnage: 1,550 tonnes.
Date of sinking: 2.21.1970.
Cause of sinking: collision against
         the shore of Le Planier.
Geographical co-ordinates:
         43°11'55" N, 5°13'42" O.
Localisation: on the rocks of
         Le Planier.
Distance from the shore:
         about 5 metres.
Minimum depth: 2 metres.
Maximum depth: 26 metres.

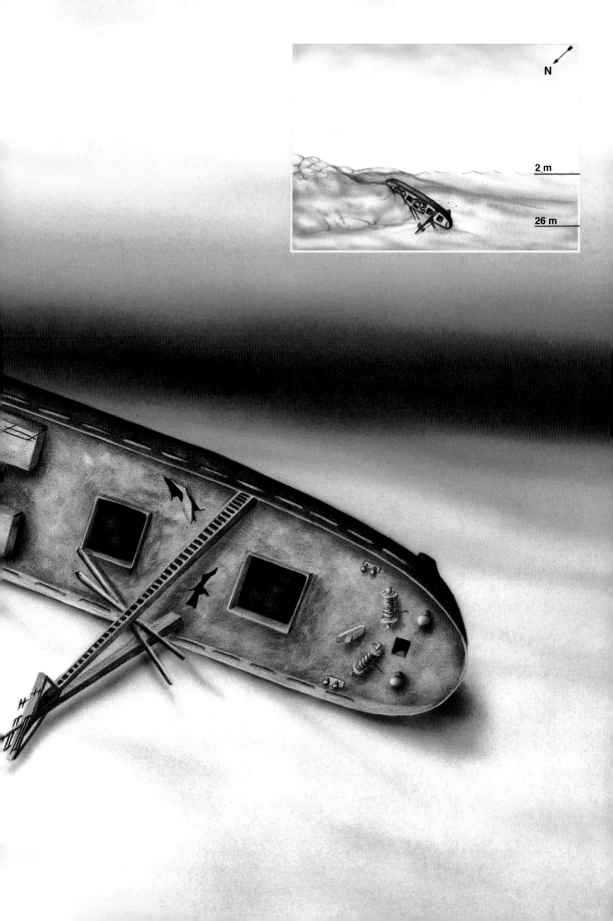

THE CHAUEN

A- The Chauen *was an elegant freighter flying the Moroccan flag and weighing 1500 tonnes.*

B - The tall main mast extends towards the surface like a gigantic claw.

The desperate message "Mayday-Mayday-Mayday-Chauen" was received by Captain Cabriel, the commander of the tug *Provençal XV*, at around 22.30 on the 21st of February, 1970. He immedia tely set course towards the site of the incident and reached the lighthouse island of Le Planier in the area in which the freighter had run aground at around midnight. The Moroccan merchant ship *Chauen* weighed 1550 tonnes and was heading for Marseilles out of Casablanca under the command of the Frenchman Captain M. Freton. There was a crew of 30 aboard and a cargo of 640 tonnes of oranges. The cause of the sinking of the *Chauen* are still unclear and shrouded in mystery given that the weather conditions were favourable and the sea was calm, even though the mistral was blowing.
The captain had already announced the ship's arrival to the harbourmaster at Marseilles and a tug was on its way to the freighter ready to guide it into the basin. Suddenly, and it has never been established whether it was a navigation error or an example of gross negligence on the part of the captain, the *Chauen* struck the rocks of the Boulevard de Dammes on the Western side of the island of Le Planier at a rate of 12 knots. The ship ran aground on the rocks and the violence of the impact and the stress imposed on the ship's structure caused a gash to open up on the starboard side of the hull. When the *Provençal XV* reached the site the *Chauen* was still afloat and it was decided that an attempt should be made to tow her off the rocks. In the meantime the atmospheric conditions had worsened considerably and it was a race against time to get the tow line aboard. After innumerable attempts to release the *Chauen* from the grip of the rocks, the tow line eventually snapped at around 2.30 in the morning. The weather

conditions were by now terrible and there was no longer any hope of salvaging the ship and the tug thus retreated. During the night a storm provided the coup de grâce and by 6 o'clock in the morning water had already filled the third hold and reached the engine-room: there was nothing to be done except leave the freighter to her tragic destiny. At 13.30 the captain ordered his crew to abandon ship and just 45 minutes later the *Chauen* rolled to port and sank. The prow still showed above the waves for the next fifteen years, but the slow, inexorable effects of erosion eventually led to a further "sinking".
The violent storms and high tides battered this section of the wreck until it too slipped beneath the surface.
The highest point of the *Chauen* can now be found at a depth of just 2 metres, directly on the

rocks. From this point the 85-metre long ships lies along the slope with the deepest section at 26 metres.

Diving to the wreck

The waters around the island of Le Planier are incredibly clear, so much so that you can admire this wreck, or at least a good part of it, from above. The *Chauen* is not particularly encrusted as it is a relatively young wreck and is lying in fairly shallow water. However, at 13 metres, sea-fans and sponges have begun to colonise the poorly lit and areas and the interiors of the holds. All the various parts of the ship are however covered with dark algae which sway gracefully to the slow rhythm of the currents. Due to the inclined position of the wreck, the objects and equipment which were in the saloons and cabins and the holds have shifted

to the deepest corners.

If you enter the wreck you will find yourself in ample and completely empty spaces with objects such as basins and lavatories arranged along the back walls as if they had been installed vertically.

It is indispensable to equip yourself with a good torch so as not to be taken by surprise by objects hidden in the dark interiors. Efficient lighting is particularly important when you explore the engine-room as there are numerous dangerous cables hanging from the walls.

I would advise you to proceed towards the starboard parapet and on towards the radar mast.

At this point you will find yourself in an area of very clear water which allows you to admire the *Chauen* in all its glory.

E

E - The wreck of the Chauen *is listing at 90° to port: consequently the starboard walls of the superstructure now appear to be almost perfectly horizontal, whilst the well preserved deck planking rises vertically. In this photo a diver is exploring the area around the radar mast.*

F - When the Chauen *eventually sank after prolonged agonies, her keel violently struck the rocks of the island of Le Planier before plunging to the sandy sea-bed. The rudder and propeller were seriously damaged during the impact.*

F

C

The vessel does not have that particular, mysterious appeal of the older wrecks, as this is a merchant ship constructed according to the modern trends in naval architecture: the bulwark, the hull, the funnel and other structural details were designed with very rounded lines according to the latest theories on streamlining. As a wreck, the *Chauen* is still too "young" and in a good state of conservation. However, thousands of fish have already taken up residence in and around her: in particular dense schools of silvery sardines hover around the superstructure, their continuous motion making the dark algae glitter. The wreck can be likened to some great monster with tangled hair reclining on the sea-bed. In spite of this rather daunting aspect, the *Chauen* dive is fairly straight forward and suitable for divers of all levels. Moreover, thanks to the fairly modest depths, the whole of the wreck can be inspected easily in one dive. The indispensable safety stops can be completed close to the wreck itself.

C - The Chauen *is to be found listing strongly to one side; the fact that she is completely covered with algae transforms an exploration of the large freighter into a surreal experience.*

D - Given that she only sank in 1970, the wreck of the Chauen *has not yet been drastically affected by the corrosive action of the salt water, and consequently much of the structure and equipment such as the capstans shown here are still well preserved.*

D

ARROYO
by Kurt Amsler

FRANCE

BANDOLO
TOULON
LA SEYNE
Cap Siciè
▼ ARROYO

FRANCE
ITALY
MEDITERRANEAN SEA

RATINGS

Location difficulty: minimum.
Visibility: usually very good.
Currents: scarce.
Diving difficulty: minimum.
Lines or nets: none.
Historical interest: low.
Photographic interest: high.
Biological interest: high.

DATA FILE

Type of wreck: support ship.
Nationality: French.
Date of construction: 1921.
Tonnage: 682 tonnes.
Date of sinking: 8.18.1953.
Cause of sinking: for training divers
        of the French Navy.
Geographical co-ordinates:
        43°2,54'4" N, 5°52,11'3" O.
Localisation: not far from the island
        of Les Deux Frères.
Distance from the shore:
        about 100 metres.
Minimum depth: 18 metres.
Maximum depth: 36 metres.

THE ARROYO

The *Arroyo*, launched in 1921, was a support ship for the French Navy equipped with enormous cisterns containing drinking water with which to supply other ships. The ship was 55 metres long, weighed 682 tonnes and was powered by an 875-hp steam engine.

In spite of its relatively humble

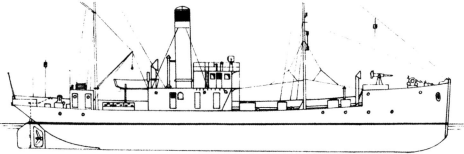

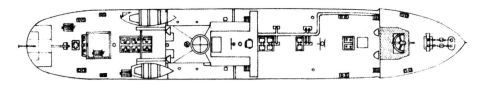

A - In this archive photograph, the Arroyo is seen at sea during an operational mission. The French naval support ship was equipped for supplying the drinking water needed by the combat vessels.

B - Fifty-five metres long, the Arroyo weighed 682 tonnes and was powered by an 875 hp steam engine. These two views show that a small defensive cannon was located at the prow. However, this weapon was removed before the ship was scuttled.

C

role, the *Arroyo* sailed as far afield as Indochina, and towards the end of its career she was based at Toulon.

In 1953 the French Navy decided to scuttle her so that she could be used for training the divers of the G.E.R.S. team (the Navy's Underwater Study and Research Group).

On the 18th of August, 1953 the *Arroyo*, under the command of Captain Philippe Taillez, was towed to her final destination: the island of Les Deux Frères, in front of Cap Sicié and not far from Toulon.

The site had been chosen by the Naval Ministry and the ship's last cargo - 20 kilos of dynamite in each cistern and 40 kilos in the engine room - proved fatal.

The explosion was very violent and unfortunately destroyed much of the ship.

According to the painstaking calculations made previously, the *Arroyo* should have sank directly to the sandy sea-bed, but due to a slight current running at the moment of the explosion part of the forward section ended up resting against a rock.

Diving to the wreck

This is a very simple dive and does not require any particular experience. You can easily explore the entire wreck which lies in an area 60 x 10 metres, and at a depth varying from 36 to 18 metres. You should also note that to the South-East of the

island of Les Deux Frères near Cap Sicié there are never any particularly strong currents and visibility is almost always excellent thanks to a favourable wind which blows from the East. As soon as you are in the water you will be able to see the two sections of the *Arroyo* lying on the sandy bottom.

The stern is the deeper of the two and has a slight list. Try looking at it from below, against the light, from which angle it is particularly impressive.

The rudder and the propeller are covered with enormous sea-fans. Try illuminating these parts of the ship with your torch: the red sea-fans in all their glory make for a truly spectacular sight. There are also some fabulous sea-fans on the quarterdeck too, on the capstans and bollards.

The open deck was not very long and, as you can see in the archive photo, the superstructure occupied almost all of the last third of the vessel.

You should note that both the superstructure and the deck have suffered from their forty-odd years of exposure to salt water, and that the ship as a whole is rather badly damaged. Nevertheless, this section of the *Arroyo* has a particular appeal and constitutes an excellent subject for spectacular underwater photography.

The forward section of the ship was destroyed, perhaps by the violence of the explosion, or though the impact against the rocks. These are, however, mere suppositions as nothing can really be established for certain with regards to this section of the wreck.

Once you have finished your exploration of the stern you find yourself swimming over a field of metal wreckage: plates, tubs and flanges probably deriving from the drinking water cisterns.

You can still see the ship's funnel, lying to the port side. It is worth pausing at the funnel and illuminating its interior.

The light of your torch will reveal a unique scene: a number of

C - The prow of the ship was damaged by the explosion and is lying on the bottom, inclined on its starboard side. You can still see the capstan and the anchors and, to the rear, part of the low platform on which the cannon was mounted.

D - Even though the Arroyo suffered considerable damage from the explosion which sent her to the bottom, and has corroded since she has been under the water, the superstructure which occupied almost the whole of the stern third of the ship is still easily recognisable.

E - The Arroyo was scuttled off the island of Les Deux Frères so as to provide a training ground for French Navy divers.

F - Splendid red gorgonians have colonised much of the twisted plating of the ship which has been lying on the sea-bed since August, 1953. In the foreground you can see two encrusted bollards.

large congers have taken up residence among the beautiful branches of the sea-fans growing in the enormous metal cylinder. As I mentioned earlier, the ship is not lying at any great depth and so you can linger longer than usual to admire the numerous examples of marine life which the *Arroyo*, in common with most wrecks, has to offer: the large scorpionfish are by no means rare, and in the spring you may see octopusses safe amidst the wreckage.

Moreover, the whole of the wreck is always patrolled by large schools of damselfish which animate the distorted structure of the vessel with flashes and reflections.

If you swim above the rocks you will find yourself in front of the prow which is lying on its starboard side in an almost vertical position, with its tip turned downwards towards the sea-bed.

The whole section is intact and you can still see the perfectly conserved capstans and bollards. Considering the continual surprises offered by the wreck and the simplicity of the dive, we would advise you to make a complete circumnavigation of the wreck and to pause to examine the details.

SAGONA
by Kurt Amsler

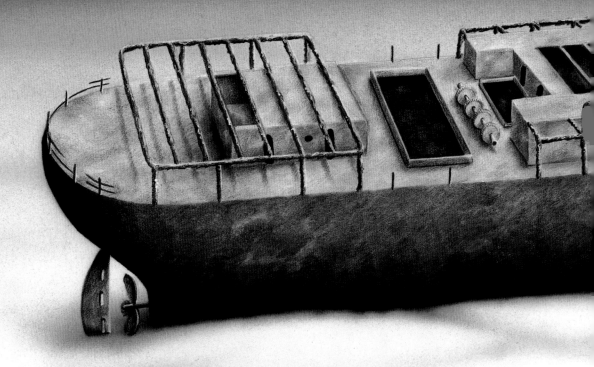

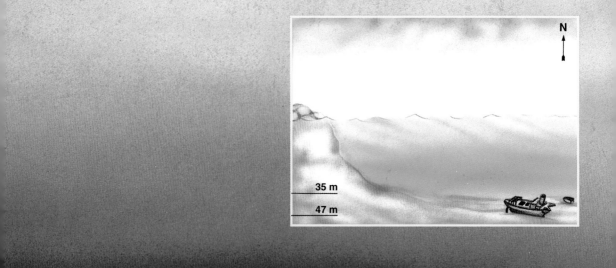

RATINGS

Location difficulty: high.
Visibility: from average to good.
Currents: often very strong.
Diving difficulty: high.
Lines or nets: none.
Historical interest: high.
Photographic interest: high.
Biological interest: high.

DATA FILE

Type of wreck: merchant ship.
Nationality: Panamese.
Date of construction: 1912.
Tonnage: 808 tonnes.
Date of sinking: 12.3.45.
Cause of sinking: mine.
Geographical co-ordinates:
      42°59'37" N, 6°16'42" O prow,
      42°59'37" N, 6°16'43" O stern.
Localisation: east of the island
      of Porquerolles.
Distance from the shore: 1.6 miles.
Minimum depth: 35 metres.
Maximum depth: 47 metres.

THE SAGONA

On the 3rd of December, 1945, the inhabitants of the island of Porquerolles were startled by the violent crash of an explosion: to the East of the island, around 1600 metres from the Petit Sarrenter, a large freighter was in flames.
The explosion had literally ripped the ship apart, splitting her into two sections; the prow could still be seen above the waves when the islanders arrived, but soon slipped beneath the surface.
The main section, swamped with vast amounts of water, sank almost immediately with the stern lifting briefly into the air before slowly and then increasingly quickly plunging into the depths.
The *Sagona* had struck one of the innumerable floating mines laid by German submarines in that stretch of sea; just two weeks earlier, a few hundred metres away, another ship had met the same end, this was the *Prosper Schiaffino*, a.k.a. the *Donator*.
The *Sagona*, now nicknamed the *Le Grec*, was built in the British yard of Dundee SB Ltd. in 1912. She was 54 metres long and 8.6 metres broad with a tonnage of 808 tonnes.
She changed hands on a number of occasions over the years: in 1914 she was sailing under the Reid Newfoundland Co.'s colours, in 1923 she was acquired by the British government whilst in 1941 she was chartered to Culliford's Associates Lines.
Finally, in 1943, the *Sagona* was flying the Panamanian flag and operated by Zarati SS Co. Ltd. The story of the sinking of the large freighter was soon largely forgotten, and it was only some time later that the French government sent a group of divers to inspect the wreck.
It was those first divers to explore the wreck who nicknamed her *Le Grec* after finding a series of documents written in Greek.

Diving to the wreck

Today the wreck of the *Sagona* is lying in two sections: the main section, with the funnel and the stern, appears to have been deliberately placed upright on the sea-bed, whilst the prow - located 60 metres further to the North - is listing at 45°.
Both sections still appear to be intact, the only extraneous element being an incredible number of red sea-fans which have literally covered available surface.
In spite of the short distance between the two sections of the ship, it is impossible to explore the whole of the wreck in one

A - The *Sagona* met the same end as the *Prosper Schiaffino*: she too was unlucky enough to strike a mine abandoned by a German submarine during the Second World War and sank almost immediately. The tragedy took place during the night of the 3rd of December, 1945.

B - The *Sagona* was a stubby freighter launched in Great Britain in 1912. She was 54 metres long and weighed 808 tonnes. The stern section of the wreck visible in this photo, is lying on sand at a depth of around 60 metres.

dive, especially as the Serranter is constantly washed by strong currents.

The principal section of the wreck, all of 40 metres long, comprises the stern of the vessel and is lying at a depth of 46 metres. The deck, the superstructure and the funnel are all close by at a similar depth.

The best way to explore this section of the wreck is to start with the propeller and the damaged rudder at the stern. You will undoubtedly be surprised by the size of the propeller blades, but you should not linger too long here so as to leave enough time for the rest of the wreck.

The quarterdeck is covered by a grating and all the structures are encrusted with algae and covered with sponges and bryozoa making for a truly spectacular composition.

After having paused to observe this natural phenomenon, you should swim above or through the superstructure and along the parapet to reach the open hatchway. There is no longer anything inside so an exploration of the interior offers little of interest and, moreover, descending to greater depths will further shorten the time you have left to explore the rest of the wreck. When conditions are favourable and visibility is good, from this part of the wreck you can already make out the funnel of the *Sagona*.

Before reaching it, however, you still have to clear the superstructure with the cabins and saloons.

You will encounter a rich variety of fauna in this part of the wreck, in particular enormous schools of sardines and groupers.

Although much was destroyed, it is worth stopping to illuminate the holds: there are large congers living in the nooks and crannies, and if you are lucky you might catch sight of groupers of notable dimensions. In this part of the wreck two small derricks point over the starboard side out towards the open sea.

They once held the lifeboats. The funnel no longer has its

original appearance, but is still impressively large and does not appear to be decaying.

From this observation point, at a depth of 35 metres you can clearly see the violence of the explosion which caused the sinking of the freighter and comprehend the drama of those terrible few minutes.

There is a distorted tangle of metalwork where the ship struck the mine, and at the point at which the hull begins to taper towards the bow its is as twisted and crumpled as a piece of screwed up paper.

Before diving to the *Sagona* you should carefully study the strength of the currents.

C - The violence of the explosion literally tore the freighter in two, devastating the deck and superstructure. The stern section, around forty metres long, is the most interesting part, partly because it is in better condition than the bow.

D - Much of the superstructure of the ship has been reduced to a skeleton of pillars and longerons, encrusted with algae, sponges and corals.

C

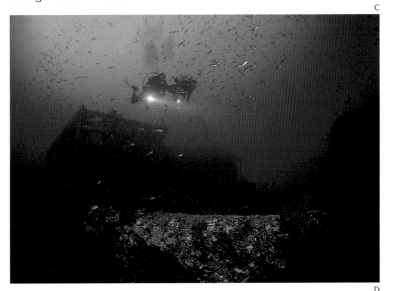

D

At times they can be so fierce as to make diving impossible; the whole dive thus needs to be planned meticulously. In certain cases the superstructure may constitute an excellent shelter from the currents. Your dive to the *Sagona* may begin either at the bow or the stern, depending on the point at which your cover boat anchors. In order to visit the bow section you should plan on a second dive. Lying at a maximum depth of 47 metres, this section of the wreck, around 20 metres long, is in good condition with the exception of the mast which once stood erect at 90° to the deck. Now its very weight, and prolonged exposure to corrosion, has caused it to collapse onto the sandy sea-bed. Innumerable vermilion sea-fans of extraordinary shapes are growing all over the wreck, around which there is a constant movement of shoals of red Anthias *(Pseudanthias squamipinnis)*. Two large groupers inhabit the interior of the prow section, although I have never personally seen them,

A - At the stern you can still see the large four-bladed propeller and the non-balanced, flat-plate rudder. You can clearly see the rudder hinge pins, arms and gudgeons in spite of the encrustation.

B - A wide variety of fauna can be seen in and around the remains of the quarter-deck, the plating of which offers a suggestive spectacle.

C- The bridge, around which swim large shoals of Anthias, is still distinguishable. The superstructure of the vessel may offer valuable shelter from the strong currents which sweep the area in which to rest for a few moments.

and conger eels up to a metre and a half in length. As with every wreck dive, you should take a good torch with you when you visit the *Sagona*. You should also remember that in the presence of strong currents it may be difficult to dive to the relatively small bow section as it offers no form of shelter. As regards equipment and personal safety, you should also remember that the wreck is lying at a considerable depth and that you will not have much time available for exploring; you cannot therefore linger over details or swim for long distances. You should consider which type of air tank would be most suitable: you will need a supply of at least 3,000 litres of air, and you should bear in mind that in strong currents you consume more air and therefore a reserve cylinder for the decompression stages would be preferable. Lastly, remember that when the strong currents are running it is better to emerge in open sea, and that it is preferable to use "parachutes" for safety stops.

E

F

G

E - The prow of the Sagona *is lying with a strong list at a depth of 46 metres. This section of the ship has been colonised by a great number of red gorgonians and is populated by dense shoals of orange Anthias.*

F - As you may deduce from the fact that the propeller aperture is virtually intact, the sandy bottom at least partially cushioned the impact.

G - The wreck of the Sagona *is literally covered with enormous examples of red gorgonians which are a sight worth diving for in their own right.*

D

D - Having transformed itself over the years into a magnificent flowering reef, the wreck of the Sagona *is now an obligatory destination for all*

enthusiasts. However, the presence of strong currents means that the dive is suitable for experts only, especially if you also want to visit the prow.

PROSPER SCHIAFFINO
by Kurt Amsler

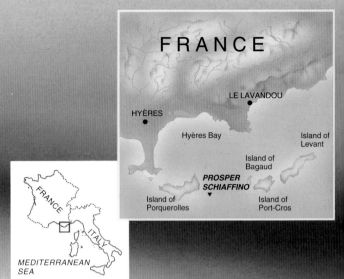

FRANCE

LE LAVANDOU

HYÈRES

Hyères Bay

Island of
Levant

Island of
Bagaud

**PROSPER
SCHIAFFINO**
▼

Island of
Porquerolles

Island of
Port-Cros

FRANCE

ITALY

MEDITERRANEAN
SEA

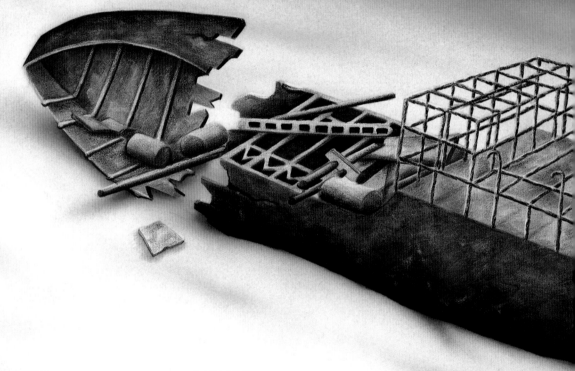

RATINGS

Location difficulty: high.
Visibility: good.
Currents: often strong.
Diving difficulty: high.
Lines or nets: none.
Historical interest: high.
Photographic interest: high.
Biological interest: high.

DATA FILE

Type of wreck: merchant ship.
Nationality: French.
Date of construction: 1931.
Tonnage: 1,698 tonnes.
Date of sinking: 11.10.1945.
Cause of sinking: mine.
Localisation: south-east of the island
        of Porquerolles.
Distance from the shore: 1 mile.
Minimum depth: 25 metres.
Maximum depth: 51 metres.

25 m

51 m

N

THE PROSPER SCHIAFFINO, A.K.A. DONATOR

A

The *Prosper Schiaffino*, also known as the *Donator*, was launched in 1931 with the name *Petite Terre* and sailed between France and the French Antilles as a banana boat. In 1939 it was acquired by the ship owner Charles Schiaffino who had the habit of naming his company's ships - which numbered around twenty - after his relations.
The Second World War was, unfortunately, fatal for Schiffino's fleet as all of his ships with the exception of the *Donator* were either sunk during the conflict or damaged whilst tied up in one port or another.
The *Donator*, in fact, came through the war unscathed, but immediately afterwards this great good fortune deserted her: on the 10th of November, 1945, the *Prosper Schiaffino*, with its cargo of wine, struck one of the many mines abandoned by German submarines and sank to the bottom. The ship, built in 1931 in the Holz Werksted A/S yards in the Norwegian port of Bergen, was 78.28 metres long, 11.94 metres broad and had a draught of 5.54 metres. She was powered by an 1,800 hp engine and had a gross tonnage of 1,698 tonnes.
In October, 1945, the ship left the port of Marseilles with a cargo of dried vegetables destined for Algeria; having reached the port of Mosatganer and completed the unloading operations, the *Donator* took on board a cargo of wine contained in countless barrels stowed in the hold and in huge tanks on the deck.
As the mine-sweeping operations in the Mediterranean had not yet been completed, the ship's commander, Captain Baillet, gave orders that a close watch be kept throughout the voyage. The *Donator* safely reached Cartegna on the Spanish coast and headed towards Toulon. With the passage between the Giens peninsula and Porquerolles blocked, she was obliged to pass

B

C

A - The Prosper Schiaffino, a merchant ship launched in Norway in 1931, was acquired by a French ship-owner eight years later, after having been used as a banana boat in the Antilles under the name Petite Terre.

B - Even though she emerged from the war unscathed, the Prosper Schiaffino was actually sunk by a mine on the 10th of November 1945. She struck the unmarked German mine and sank to the bottom in just a few minutes.

C - Today, the Prosper Schiaffino has been transformed into a underwater garden lying on the sandy sea-bed off the island of Porquerolles.

the island to the South. It was the 10th of November, and a strong mistral wind was blowing.
The freighter, slowed by the weight of its cargo, struggled to make headway against waves which were breaking over her decks. Off the South-East point of the island, the *Donator* turned to pass between Porquerolles and Port Cros.

Calamity struck at ten past one in the afternoon. An enormous explosion rocked the whole ship, tearing apart the prow: she had struck a mine that had either been drifting or was still anchored to the sea-bed and had yet to be discovered by the minesweepers. A few seconds after the explosion the ship had already begun to take on huge quantities of water

52

and the stern began to rise. The 29 crew members tried to lower the boats, but the worsening position of the ship rendered the operation impossible. Some of the men panicked and dived into the sea, others tried to launch at least the cork rafts secured on deck. This all took place in the space of a few minutes whilst the stern rose ever higher: by the time the propeller was exposed to the air the *Donator* was condemned. The seamen who had managed to swim clear of the zone or had managed to climb aboard the raft saw their vibrating ship plunge to the depths, accompanied by a sinister clamour. A British naval aircraft on a recconnaisance flight saw the incident and reported back to its base and four hours later help reached the survivors. Two men were lost and 27 were rescued, two of whom never regained consciousness.

The sinking of the *Donator* represented the loss of Charles Schiaffino and Company's last ship.

D - A large spare propeller, now completely encrusted, is still fixed to the superstructure at the stern.

E - As you can see in this photograph, the long years spent at the bottom of the sea have transformed this ship into a flowering "garden" of rare beauty.

F - Transformed into a multi-coloured reef, the wreck is covered with magnificent gorgonians, among which swim orange Anthias and shoals of other small, coloured fish.

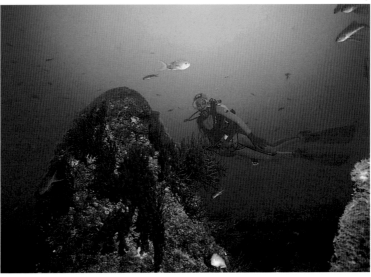

Diving to the wreck

The wreck of the *Donator* today
lies on a sandy sea-bed; the bow
section ripped apart by the
explosion is to be found at a depth
of 48 metres, whilst the stern is at
51 metres. The deck is at 40
metres and the highest parts of the
superstructure are at a depth of 35
metres. The tip of the mast is 25
metres from the surface. The wreck
is fairly large and so a complete
exploration is rarely possible.
A complete circumnavigation of
the freighter can only be made
when the currents are very weak,
and favourable conditions such as
these are very rare. If you plan
your dive to the wreck of the
Donator carefully it will be an
unforgettable experience.
The fifty years spent beneath the
waves have, in fact, transformed
the wreck into a "flowering" reef.
Ideal conditions have been created
for the development of colonies of
a wide variety of marine
organisms. Along the flanks of the
ship, multi-coloured sea-fans have
literally covered the plates, whilst
around the superstructure live
schools of brightly coloured little fish.
The holds are characterised by the
continuous undulating movement
of the small orange Anthias
(Pseudanthias squamipinnis).
Of course, you will also find all the
other species which usually
colonise the wrecks. The stern is
undoubtedly the most interesting
area. In this section you can clearly
see the large propeller and rudder
covered in huge sea-fans.
Moreover, you can still see the
large ship's wheel and, in front of
the lowest section of the
superstructure, a spare propeller
still fixed in position. Swimming
alongside the four blades of the
propeller you get a clear indication
of the kind of thrust necessary to
propel a ship of this size. The entire
forecastle is lying at a slightly
greater depth. The deck plates
have been detached and you can
thus look freely into the hold; the
light of your torch will reveal
numerous metal barrels scattered
amidst masses of wreckage. In the
centre of the quarterdeck stands
the mainmast, the tip of which is

A

B

C

A - The long period
spent under the
water has reduced
the superstructure
of the ship to a
metal skeleton
to which a great
number of red
gorgonians have
attached
themselves.

B - The stern is the
most interesting
section of the
wreck: here divers
can easily examine
the rudder and the
great four-bladed
propeller covered
with gigantic red
gorgonians.

C - The deck
planking has
rotted, leaving the
underlying metal
structures exposed
and allowing you
to look into the
hold.

25 metres from the surface.
At this point you are faced with
what remains of the superstructure:
the ribs and the partially perforated
walls. In order to continue your
dive you can turn back towards the
stern, or towards the starboard side
of the ship passing through the
superstructure. To the right and
left you will see the lifeboat hoists.
The compressed base amidships
area is all that remains of the
funnel. The walls of what was
once the bridge falls suddenly and
steeply towards the forecastle.
In this area you can see a number
of loading derricks set transversally
to the deck gratings. The large
metal cylinders located here and
which you can also see in the hold
area were perhaps the tanks

*D - In order to dive
safely to the
Prosper Schiaffino
you need to bear
in mind the
considerable depth
at which the wreck
is lying, and the
frequently strong
currents. If you take
the necessary
precautions, the
dive will be a
thrilling adventure.*

*E - The explosion
of the mine which
struck the Prosper
Schiaffino was
extremely violent
and sank the vessel
almost
immediately.
During the dive
you will see that
the forward third
of ship was reduced
to a mass of
distorted scrap.*

*F - The main mast,
only partially
mutilated, rises to
a point 25 metres
form the surface.
Since the wreck is
fairly large and the
currents are often
tricky, you are
advised not to
complete the
exploration of the
vessel in a single
dive unless the
conditions are
particularly
favourable.*

containing the wine. It is in this
section of the wreck that you get
an idea of the intensity of the
explosion: a tangle of distorted
plates distinguishes the bow
section lying on its port side with
the prow buried in the sand.
You should carefully certain
aspects to ensure a safe dive to the
Donator: it is a large wreck lying at
a considerable depth and in waters
characterised by strong currents.
If you want to make a longer dive,
however, you can remain close to
the deck of the ship. You will need
the usual equipment advisable for
deep dives in the Mediterranean
and we would advise a supply of
at least 3,000 litres of air.

TANTINE
by Kurt Amsler

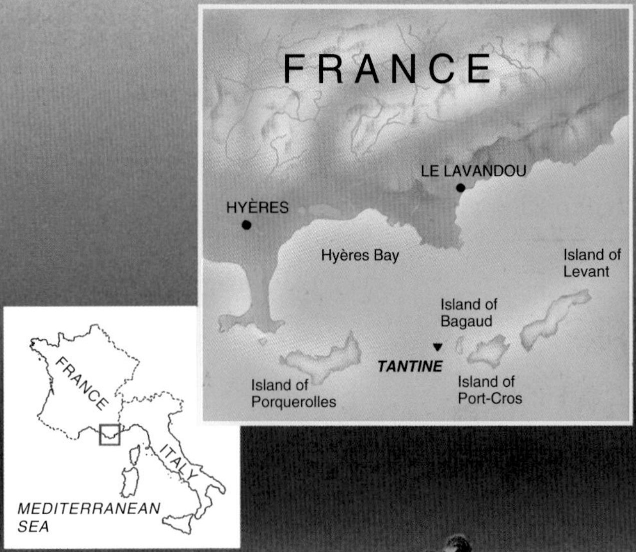

FRANCE

LE LAVANDOU

HYÈRES

Hyères Bay

Island of
Levant

Island of
Bagaud

▼ *TANTINE*

Island of
Porquerolles

Island of
Port-Cros

FRANCE

ITALY

MEDITERRANEAN
SEA

RATINGS

Location difficulty: high.
Visibility: from good to very good.
Currents: often strong.
Diving difficulty: from average to high.
Lines or nets: none to disturb
     the dive.
Historical interest: low.
Photographic interest: high.
Biological interest: high.

DATA FILE

Type of wreck: heavy tug
Nationality: French.
Date of construction: unknown.
Tonnage: unknown.
Date of sinking: unknown.
Cause of sinking: bad weather.
Geographical co-ordinates:
     43°1'28" N, 6°21'40" O
Localisation: north-west of the
     Island of Bagaud.
Distance from the shore:
     about 600 metres.
Minimum depth: 45 metres.
Maximum depth: 48 metres.

THE TANTINE

Virtually nothing is known of the history and provenance of the "congers wreck" at Port-Cros. Almost certainly she was a heavy tug with a derrick installed on her stern. Both the date and the cause of the sinking are unknown, but it is said that the tug was towing a barge to one port or another, and that during this operation the heavy swell, or the sudden shifting of the numerous bricks she was carrying severely compromised her stability and safety. So as not to lose the barge too, the towing line was released and the tug was abandoned to its destiny. The *Tantine* is around 20 metres long and 6 metres wide; the derrick is located on a kind of platform around three metres high, with its arm lying across the deck. The forward section of the vessel is flat, and parts of the bulwark have collapsed.

The port side of the tug is covered with a fishing net. Throughout the wreck you will see countless bricks, but quite why they were aboard is unknown; perhaps they were either part of the cargo or served as ballast.

The *Tantine* is now lying at a depth of 48 metres off the island of Bagaud, within the Port Cros Underwater Park.

A

B

C

A - Presumably the Tantine, a heavy tug equipped with a derrick, sank off Port-Cros whilst it was towing a barge. The incident was perhaps caused by the instability of the tug's cargo which compromised the vessel's trim and led to her capsizing.

B - The massive derrick was installed at the stern on a kind of raised platform as wide as the boat itself. The arm, which was once resting on the deck, has now definitively collapsed.

C - The Tantine is rightly known as the "congers wreck" due to the numerous examples of the species which have taken up residence here.

Diving to the wreck

The principal appeal of this wreck is not so much the vessel itself as its inhabitants. The *Tantine* is lying on a sandy sea-bed and thus it should come as no surprise that so many fish have taken up residence. The most spectacular inhabitants are undoubtedly the congers which grow to lengths of up to 3 metres and may weigh as much as 65 kilos. Their colouring varies from grey-brown to black with a number of blue patches and a lighter belly.
The long branchial openings stretch from the belly to the pectoral fins. The congers are characterised by an unusual snout with a slightly protruding lower jaw; they generally live on shallow and rocky bottoms where the sea is calm, but they can also be encountered at considerable depths. These fish usually occupy their dens during the day, venturing out only occasionally in order to observe what is happening around them; during the night, on the other hand, they emerge to hunt for food, in particular crustaceans, bottom feeders and cuttlefish which form their staple diet.
During your dive to the *Tantine* you should not have to look far for these unusual fish as they have chosen all the various nooks and crannies in the stern section where the derrick is to be found as their personal domain.
All you need to do is illuminate the area under the derrick platform and you will be faced countless round black eyes. The congers do not always leave their dens and swim freely; however, when they do and you manage to see them in all their agile elegance, you will realise just how large they are. Many are over two metres long. You should not be intimidated by the size of these fish, nor should you be alarmed or show that you are nervous when they approach you out of curiosity.
You should avoid carrying any form of bait with you when you dive - dead fish for example - as you need considerable experience to be able to feed these enormous

eels safely. The congers' jaws are formidable and when they feed they behave unpredictably: you therefore run the risk of being bitten. You will also see other fish on the *Tantine* apart from the congers: large, solemn scorpionfish swim around the platform, for example, whilst below the plating there are a number of silvery *Phycis blennoides*, characterised by their long barbels.
Around the wreck you will usually see great schools of sardines which enliven and illuminated the depths with their flashing silvery reflections.

The stern area is dominated by the orange of the minuscule *Anthias (Pseudanthias squamipinnis)*.
In order to observe this magnificent world without any problems you should keep your distance from the sea-bed so as to avoid disturbing the sand. You should also bear in mind that the *Tantine* is lying at a considerable depth and both your descent and ascent take place in the open sea in an area subject to strong currents; it is therefore a wreck for expert divers with experience of diving in currents.

D

E

D - The conger eels (Conger conger) are bony fish very common in the Mediterranean. They are nocturnal, inhabit protected recesses and feed mainly on small crustaceans.

E - There are numerous residents of the wreck well over 2 metres long: although the congers are generally peaceful, their curiosity can often cause problems for divers. You should avoid brusque movements and, above all, avoid trying to feed them.

THE GRUMMAN F4F-4 WILDCAT OF LE LAVANDOU
by Kurt Amsler

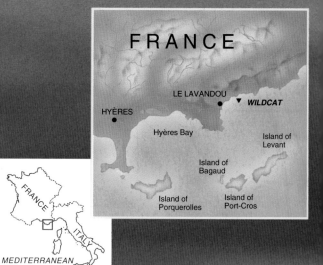

FRANCE

LE LAVANDOU
HYÈRES ▼ WILDCAT
Hyères Bay
Island of Levant
Island of Bagaud
Island of Porquerolles
Island of Port-Cros

FRANCE
ITALY
MEDITERRANEAN SEA

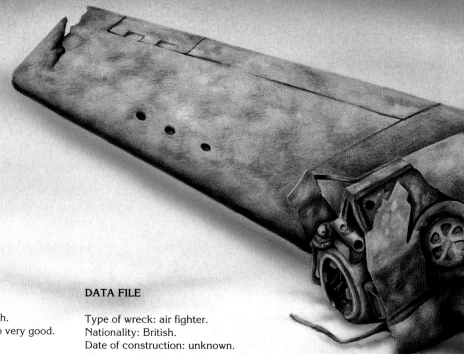

RATINGS

Location difficulty: high.
Visibility: from good to very good.
Currents: scarce.
Diving difficulty: high.
Lines or nets: none.
Historical interest: high.
Photographic interest: high.
Biological interest: average.

DATA FILE

Type of wreck: air fighter.
Nationality: British.
Date of construction: unknown.
Wingspan: 11.58 metres.
Lenght: 8.76 metres.
Weight at take off: 3.360 kilos.
Date of sinking: unknown.
Cause of sinking: crashed or thrown
    into the sea due to a
    technical fault.
Geographical co-ordinates:
    43°6'15" N, 6°23'75" O.
Localisation: in front of a Formigue
    du Lavandou.
Distance from the shore: 3.5 miles.
Minimum depth: 51 metres.
Maximum depth: 53 metres.

51 m

53 m

N

THE GRUMMAN F4F-4 WILDCAT

A

B

A - This archive
photograph shows
a number of
Wildcats ready for
take-off on an
American aircraft
carrier. The small
Grumman fighter
bore the brunt of
the operations in
the Pacific theatre
during the first two
years of the war.

B - Agile, powerful
and well armed,
the Wildcat was
one of the most
common carrier-
borne fighters of the
Second World War.
In this photograph
you can see the
retractable
undercarriage
which was housed
entirely within the
fuselage.

C

The *Grumman F4F-4 Wildcat*
was used as both a fighter and
a bomber.
The aircraft was originally built
in America, but in the immediate
pre- and post-war years it was
also assembled in Great Britain,
and the Royal Navy possessed
1,213 examples known by the
name *Martlet*.
These planes were powered
by a Pratt and Whitney 1,200
hp engine providing them with
a maximum speed of 512 kph,
an operational ceiling of around
11,000 metres, and a range
of over 1,200 km.
They were armed with six
machine-guns and two 45-kg
bombs. Little is known of the
background to this wreck; the
plane carries British markings
and is possible to decipher the
script Royal Navy.
The French wreck specialist,
J. P. Joncheray has suggested
that this *Wildcat* might be one of
the 220 examples seconded to
France by Great Britain following
the war.
It is possible that the plane was
carried on the aircraft carrier
Hermes which frequently cruised
in this area, and that it was thrown
into the sea as it was too badly
damaged to be repaired.
This system of disposing of
unwanted airframes was much
in vogue in that period.
However, the retracted position
of the undercarriage contradicts
this hypothesis and leads one to
suspect that the plane actually
crashed into the sea due to a
technical fault. There is, however,
no hard evidence to confirm
either theory.

Diving to the wreck

The wreck of the *Wildcat* is to be
found East-South-East of
Formigue du Lavandou at a depth
of around 53 metres, and lies
upside down on a sandy sea-bed.
It has a wingspan of 11.58 metres
and the fuselage is 8.76 metres
long. The water in this area,
around 3.5 miles from the port
of Le Lavandou, is usually clear,
and the wreck is visible from a
depth of about 30 metres.

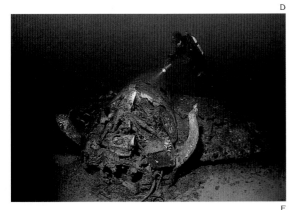

D

although the blades are now distorted. In spite of the limited time available, it is still sufficient to explore this wreck in its entirety; however it is a dive suitable for experts only due to the considerable depth. There is no need to swim any great distance once you reach the bottom as you anchor practically above the wreck. We would nevertheless advise you to dive with a supply of 3,000 litres of air.

C - A diver illuminating the tail-plane of the Le Lavandou Wildcat; at the top, left, you can see the tail wheel, still fitted with its tyre.

D - The Wildcat is lying upside down on the sandy sea-bed; the nose section of the plane is badly damaged and reduced to a tangle of cables and distorted metalwork.

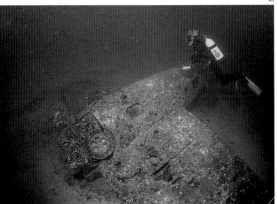

E

F

E - At the end of the war, a number of Wildcats employed by the Royal Navy were seconded by Great Britain to France. They were then used at length on the French aircraft carriers. It has been suggested that the Le Lavandou aircraft was in service on the Hermes and that she was ditched overboard when found to be irreparably damaged. However, the fact that the plane's undercarriage is retracted arouses some doubts. It could hardly have retracted after the crash, and it would necessarily have been lowered to allow the aircraft to be manoeuvred on the deck of the ship. It is therefore possible that the Wildcat actually crashed close to the aircraft carrier.

Whilst you are exploring the remains of the aircraft you should be careful not to disturb the sand as suspended sediment will seriously reduce visibility. You should carefully adjust your buoyancy so that you can hover just above the wreck and thus examine it in detail.

The *Wildcat* is particularly interesting in that it is practically intact. Only the nose has suffered any serious damage, and the cockpit is now uncovered.

Still taking care how you fin so as to avoid raising sand, you can illuminate the area below the wings in which you will be able to observe congers and scorpionfish, the typical fish found around wrecks. The are many large yellow spiral tube-worms on the tail making an attractive contrast with the infinite blue of the sea.

The engine can be seen trapped below the tail-plane, evidently torn from its housing when the wreck was violently wrenched at some point.

The propeller is still in place,

G

F - The fighter large engine was probably wrenched off when the wreck was dragged at some point, and is now lying beneath the tail-plane.

G - The engine's three-bladed propeller is still fixed to the hub. The Pratt & Whitney 1,200 hp radial engine provided the aircraft with a maximum speed of 512 kph.

TOGO
by Kurt Amsler

RATINGS

Location difficulty: high.
Visibility: good.
Currents: scarce.
Diving difficulty: high.
Lines or nets: none.
Historical interest: average.
Photographic interest: average.
Biological interest: average.

DATA FILE

Type of wreck: merchant ship.
Nationality: Italian.
Date of construction: 1882.
Tonnage: 1,640 tonnes.
Date of sinking: 5.12.1918.
Cause of sinking: mine.
Geographical co-ordinates:
43°10,14'0" N, 6°16,26'3" O.
Localisation: west of Point Dubreuil,
in the Cavalaire bay.
Distance from the shore: about
1,000 metres.
Minimum depth: 45 metres.
Maximum depth: 60 metres.

A

The *Togo*, launched in 1882, was built by Robert Thompson and Sons of Newcastle in England. Bought by the Compagnie Havraise Peninsulaire, she was baptised *Ville de Valence* and was used to transport lemons from Spain. In 1906 the vessel was sold to an Italian ship-owner from Savona who changed her name to *Amor*. Subsequently she was sold once again to a Genoan company and, in 1912, was once again renamed as the *Togo*.
The imposing steamship was now used for transporting coal. The *Togo* was built during a watershed period for naval architecture and thus boasted a number of innovative features: she was built in steel, had five watertight bulkheads and a double hull. She had three masts providing a broad expanse of canvas but was also equipped with a powerful engine.
The *Togo* was 76 metres long, 10.35 metres broad, weighed 1,640 tonnes and carried a crew of 28. In spite of the numerous threats faced by the ship, she came through the First World War unscathed. However, it was a mine laid by the German submarine *UC-35* which was responsible for the *Togo*'s eventual demise. Six months after the end of the war, on the 12th of May, 1918, she struck the mine and sank to the bottom of the Bay of Cavalaire. The wreck lay forgotten on the sea-bed for some considerable time, abandoned to its tragic destiny. In spite of the fact that the fishermen of Cavalaire trawling the rich waters of the sheltered bay occasionally found their nets ripped, nobody was curious enough to descend to see what "mysteries" were hidden at the bottom of the sea.
All that was known was that in that area lay wreck of the Ramon Membru - nobody was aware of a second vessel. Once the biologist and diver Richard Calme came to hear of these strange facts he

A - The Togo, was the product of transitional technology: of all-metal construction,

she was powered by a steam engine, but also had three masts for sailing under canvas.

began to investigate the phenomenon and, in the April of 1977, had the local fishermen take him to the site and made his first dives. It is easy to imagine his shock and surprise when instead of the expected reef he was faced with the wreck of a ship lying upright on the sea-bed.
He was the first man to admire what is a veritable phenomenon of nature: the hull of an unknown ship encrusted with the most extraordinary forms of life.
Over the course of the years numerous objects have been recovered from the wreck and these have allowed us to discover the provenance of the ship, and confirm that it actually was the *Ville de Valence* or *Togo* which met her destiny in the waters off Cavalaire.

Diving to the wreck

In my opinion, the *Togo* is one of the most attractive and greatest wrecks in the whole of the Mediterranean. It is around 60 metres long but it is no longer

intact: the propeller and around a ten-metre length of the stern are to be found some distance from the main section of the wreck and lying at a depth of 60 metres. The vessel is lying upright on the sandy bottom; the highest elements on the deck are at a depth of 47 metres, whilst the prow is at 55 metres. Divers immersed in the darkness of the depths where only very weak sunlight manages to penetrate, will be taken aback by the looming presence of the ship. The *Togo* appears to be enormous, in fact, and it is also completely covered with delicate sea-fans, whilst dense schools of fish swim through the structures creating a quite extraordinary scene. You would be well advised to concentrate on the apertures along the deck as the high flanks and the surrounding sandy sea-bed have little of interest. Moreover, descending any deeper would only reduce the time you have available for exploring the wreck. You should begin your dive at the prow: to the right and left

B

B - A diver illuminating the duct leading from a ventilator; in the foreground you can see the great elliptical aperture where the funnel once stood.

of the capstan you will find the two anchors still attached to chains hanging along the ship's sides. The bow is fairly pointed and the sides of the ship descend vertically for about 8 metres. As you continue to inspect this area you will note certain minor superstructure elements at the prow of the *Togo* with rounded windows on their upper part. Your exploration continues with the forecastle with its large loading hatches. The holds can be lit with your torch, but it is not advisable to enter them as, apart from the remains of the coal carried as cargo, there is nothing left to see. There are around 20 metres between the forecastle and the superstructure at the centre of the ship, and you can go to the right or left, passing beneath an arcade of sea-fans. This natural wonder is so suggestive that it is worthy of examination from both sides. In the centre there is a large aperture where the great funnel once stood; whilst both to port and starboard you can see the lifeboat hoists equally covered in splendid red sea-fans. Inside the superstructure you can still see common objects such as bathtubs and sanitary equipment. You can see a mast lying across the starboard side of the ship. As you move a few metres further towards the stern you find that the wreck has been sharply truncated. Almost as if they had been snapped in the enormous fists of a submarine giant, the flanks of ship open towards the infinite blue expanse of the sea. You should, of course, plan your dive to the *Togo* very carefully, bearing in mind above all else your personal safety and precisely calculating the length of time you have available. It is a large ship and, furthermore, you will need to adjust your buoyancy and ballast carefully. If you want to complete a circumnavigation of the hull, you must stay at deck level otherwise you risk running out of time. You should also remember to keep a careful check on your air supply so as to avoid any problems at this depth.

C

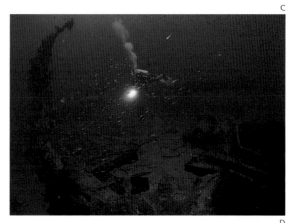

D

E

F

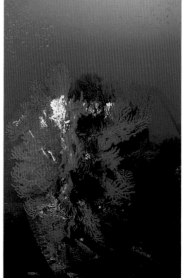

C - Behind the diver you can see a mast lying over the starboard side of the ship, to the right is a capstan, whilst on the left you can see a life-boat hoist.

D - In certain areas the plates of the Togo have been completely covered by colonies of gorgonians.

E - Attracted by the steps leading down into the ship, a diver scans the opening of a hatchway with the beam of his torch.

F - The Togo is almost completely covered with red gorgonians which transform what is already a suggestive dive into an unforgettable adventure.

RUBIS
by Kurt Amsler

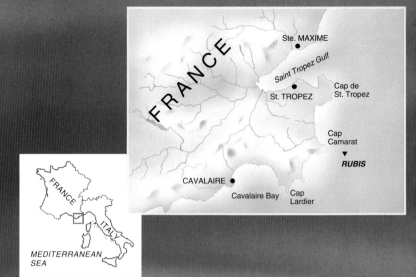

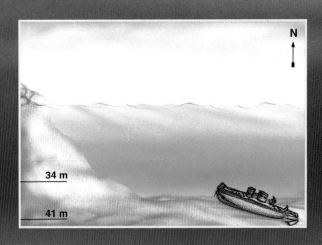

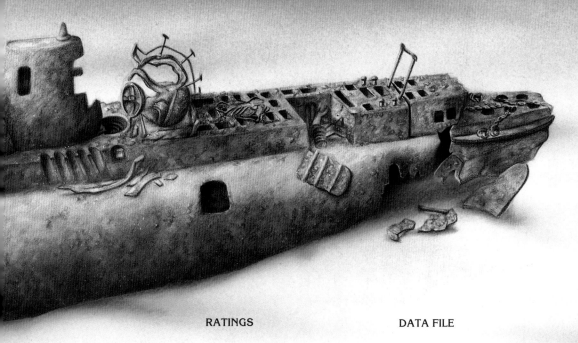

RATINGS

Location difficulty: high.
Visibility: from good to very good.
Currents: sometimes very strong.
Diving difficulty: high.
Lines or nets: none.
Historical interest: high.
Photographic interest: high.
Biological interest: average.

DATA FILE

Type of wreck: mining submarine.
Nationality: French.
Date of construction: 1931.
Tonnage: 762 tonnes.
Date of sinking: 1.31.1958.
Cause of sinking: sunken as training
    vessel for French Navy divers.
Geographical co-ordinates:
    43°11'37" N, 6°42'10" O.
Localisation: not far from
    Cap Camarat.
Distance from the shore: 1.4 miles.
Minimum depth: 34 metres.
Maximum depth: 41 metres.

A

B

C

The French submarine *Rubis* was designed in 1925, launched in 1931 and commissioned in 1932. Built in the Toulon yards, the *Rubis* was the fourth of a series of six submarines. The class prototype, the *Saphir*, was built in 1930 and was followed by *Turquoise, Nautilus, Rubis, Diamant* and, in 1937, *Perle*. This class of submarine was designed so that it could lay mines in enemy territory without having to surface, and could also launch torpedoes.

All of the 32 mines carried by the submarine were housed outside the principal pressurised compartment but within the hydrodynamic hull.

Each of 8 wells on either side of the boat contained 2 mines, one on top of the other. Having reached the designated target zone, the submarine released the mines via a compressed air system. It was necessary to rapidly counter the loss of the weight of the mine so as to avoid surfacing suddenly in enemy territory.

A - This historic photograph shows the Rubis *cruising in the waters off Toulon. Following the vessel's glorious service during the Second World War, she was transferred to the French port and was used as a floating school for cadet submariners until 1958.*

B, E - These drawings of the Rubis, *the fourth of a series of six submarines, reveals her perfect, modern, and very hydrodynamic lines.*

C - Two Schweizer Oerlicher cannons were installed on the Rubis*'s deck as vital anti-aircraft defences.*

Older submarines released their mines through a hatch; with the new externally located system there was less risk of unwanted surfacing.

The mines were manufactured by Sauter & Harley and contained no less than 220 kilograms of explosive. After having been positioned, these instruments of death and destruction automatically rose to the surface and were firmly anchored by a chain. The submarine's four-stroke, six-cylinder engines were produced by Vickers-Armstrong and boasted power outputs of 650 hp. The vessel used two Schneider electric motors when submerged which gave it a maximum speed of 8 knots. The *Rubis* could dive to a depth of 50 metres and operate at a

periscope depth of 15 metres. Two Schweizer Oerlicher cannons were installed on the deck and the *Rubis* was also armed with five torpedoes which could be launched from the stern.

Initially all six submarines were stationed at Toulon, but in 1936 the *Rubis* was despatched to Cherbourg so that its crew could train in laying mines in the depths of the Atlantic Ocean.

Early in 1939 the vessel was sent back to the Mediterranean and stationed in the Tunisian port of Bizerte, then a French colony. Later it was attached to the 9th Submarine Fleet based at Dundee in Scotland. The *Rubis*, under the command of Captain Georges Cabanier, received her first orders from the French admiralty early in 1940. They concerned an allied operation with the aim of protecting the Finnish coastline in the event of an attack by the Russians. Unexpectedly on the 9th of April the German Wehrmacht invaded Denmark and Norway and the allies immediately began operations to mine the Norwegian

D - The commander of the French submarine, Georges Cabanier scrutinising the horizon through the vessel's periscope.

The Rubis was capable of diving to a depth of 50 metres and could operate at a periscope depth of 15 metres.

F - Life on board was harsh and restrictive, but there was a lighter side. The photograph shows a small dog, the vessel's mascot.

G - Two sailors are involved in checking the torpedo tubes.

A

B

the 24th of the same month, the vessel was sequestered by the British. Whilst it maintained the same crew and captain it continued to fight on behalf of the French resistance under the British flag.

Examination of certain documents relating to the military operations has revealed that in the course of 28 missions the submarine laid 683 mines which caused the sinking of 15 tenders, 7 patrol boats and a 4,360-tonne freighter, as well as seriously damaging a submarine.

At the end of the war the *Rubis* returned in triumph to Toulon where the crew members were decorated with highest French and British honours. Following a complete refit the *Rubis* continued to be used by the French Navy for some years as a training vessel.

In 1950 it was transformed into a floating school for cadet submariners, and was later used as a target in sonar exercises.

At the end of her long and glorious career the *Rubis* was spared the indignity of being broken up.

She was scuttled on the 31st of January, 1956 off Cap Camarat, between Cavalaire and St. Tropez, thus conserving a page in the

A - This photograph captures a typical moment aboard the submarine: two sailors are examining a control panel.

B - This shot illustrates the heart of the Rubis: *the engine room. The submarine's six-cylinder, four-stroke engine was manufactured by Vickers-Armstrong. When submerged the boat was propelled by two Schneider electric motors.*

C - General De Gaulle reviewing the crew of the Rubis. *At the end of the war the submarine, which had mainly operated in the Mediterranean and the North Sea, returned to Toulon where its entire crew was decorated with the highest French and British honours.*

waters to try to block the transport of steel and other metals indispensable to the German war effort. All the available submarines were used in this operation.

On the 3rd of May the *Rubis* and other vessels mined the entrance to the Egersund Fjord on the Norwegian coast.

After two further missions in the same waters the French Admiralty recalled all its vessels involved in the mine-laying operations.

Only the *Rubis* remained to complete one last mission - the mining of the Trondheim Fjord in which a significant part of the German North Sea Fleet was anchored. Following the signing of the armistices between France and Germany on 22nd of June, and between France and Italy on

C

turbulent history of the twentieth century. The wreck has proved to be of particular interest; so much so that it has attracted countless divers over the years.

Moreover it also continues to perform an important military role as a target for the sonar equipment used by naval ships during exercises.

Diving to the wreck

The *Rubis* can now be found lying upright on a sandy seabed at a depth of 40 metres, almost as if it had been deliberately positioned. In spite of the considerable depth, when the water is clear the wreck can almost be seen from the surface. The wreck of the *Rubis* is surrounded by a halo of mystery and divers are immediately struck by a sense of awe.

The position of the wreck perhaps accentuates this impression: the submarine is lying on its keel, almost as if it were ready to launch an attack on an unseen enemy. There really is a sense that from one moment to the next the *Rubis*'s electric motors might start up and that it could sail off into the distance.

The wreck is still in good condition, even though many components such as the conning tower, the gun platform and the covers over the bays housing the mines have irremediably corroded. The plates of the *Rubis* are not as heavily covered with vegetation as those of the wreck of the *Togo* located close by.

D

E

D - A diver illuminating the cable cutter; still a feature of the French submarine's prow.

E - The Rubis*'s conning tower is still in good condition and is thus perfectly recognisable. Today it is surrounded numerous Anthias (Pseudanthias squamipinnis).*

A

A - In this photograph you can see the stern of the French submarine Illuminated by a diver: the light shows it is still intact.

B - This photograph shows the plates of the Rubis *which, in contrast with the majority of the Mediterranean wrecks, have not been encrusted with submarine vegetation.*

B

C

C - Through the rents in the hull of the Rubis *caused by the detachment of a number of plates, you can see the water-filled cavity between the inner and outer hulls which allowed the trim and depth of the submarine to be adjusted.*

D - Like a sleeping giant, the Rubis *lies upright on the sandy seabed almost as if it were waiting for an order to start up its engines and depart for a new mission.*

D

F

G

H

E, F - Diving to the Rubis is a truly unique experience which, especially when exploring all the various details from the conning tower to the mine wells, from the torpedo tubes to the elevators, brings to life the most glorious episodes in the career of this pride of the French Navy.

G - The open hatch appears to invite the diver to penetrate the interior of the submarine and uncover its innermost secrets; in reality the passage is too narrow to enter with breathing gear and, furthermore, visiblity inside is virtually zero due to the considerable sedimentation.

H - A diver pauses at the stern of the submarine near the trim tanks which allowed the vessel to be maintained in a horizontal position.

Sea fans and sponges can be found on the flanks of the submarine, whilst the torpedo tubes, the cracks and the niches house enormous conger eels, moray eels and scorpionfish. However, divers will not be attracted by the spectacular forms of life inhabiting the *Rubis* so much as by the conning tower, the mine housings, the elevator and the cable cutter on the bow. If visitors to the wreck, captivated by the strange fascination it exudes, examine these details closely they will be able, albeit briefly, to revive the vessel and to "see" it engaged in one of those glorious missions which preceded its final anchorage on the seabed. The appeal and the spectacle of the *Rubis* should not distract divers from safety procedures, however.
Dives should be programmed carefully.
The wreck is 66 metres long and it is thus possible to explore both sides in a single dive.
It is not advisable to enter the submarine through the narrow hatch, firstly because 15-litre tanks or twin tanks are too bulky, and secondly because visibility is virtually zero due to heavy sediment.
Furthermore, it should be remembered that in certain periods of the year and at certain times of the day there are strong currents around Cap Camarat. These factors should be taken into consideration before making the dive.

THE ANTHÉOR BARGES
by Kurt Amsler

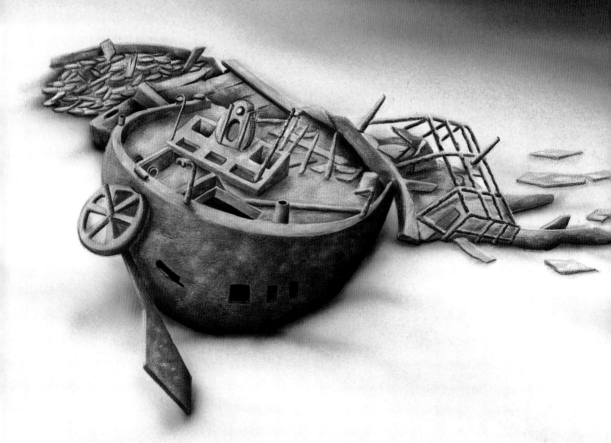

RATINGS

Location difficulty: average.
Visibility: good.
Currents: scarce.
Diving difficulty: average.
Lines or nets: none.
Historical interest: high.
Photographic interest: high.
Biological interest: high.

DATA FILE

Type of wreck: river barges.
Nationality: French.
Date of construction: unknown.
Tonnage: 352 tonnes the *Jean Luzon*,
        338 tonnes the *St. Antoine*.
Date of sinking: 1.31.1944.
Cause of sinking: torpedo.
Geographical co-ordinates:
        45°25'38" N, 6°54'35" O
Localisation: in front of the beacon
        of Ballise de la Chretienne.
Distance from the shore: 0.9 miles.
Minimum depth: 26 metres.
Maximum depth: 36 metres.

THE ANTHÉOR BARGES

During the Second World War barges were used to transport the munitions destined for the German troops occupying France.
These vessels were designed for use on rivers, in particular the Seine and the Loire, and were therefore completely unsuited to sailing on the open sea.
The war, however, forced them to shuttle between Marseilles and Genoa, hugging the coastline all the way. Their cargoes always comprised explosives, and these particular barges were loaded to gunwales with ammunition and heavy artillery shells. Thanks to these cargoes, which were as important to the German army as they were highly dangerous, the barges were escorted by heavily armed support ships or by aircraft. The barges themselves were usually fitted with anti-aircraft machine-guns at the stern.

These precautions were insufficient, however, to protect the Jean Suzon and the St. Antoine: on the 31st of January, 1944, their convoy was spotted by a submarine in the Ballise de la Chretienne area between Agay and Anthéor. There was no escape for the barges, and at 11.30 they were struck by three torpedoes and sank within a few minutes. A fourth torpedo missed its target and exploded against the rocks. It was recently discovered that the submarine was the British vessel, H.M.S. Untiring.
The following laconic words can be read in the log kept by the occupying German admiralty: "31st of January, 1944, morning mist, winds weak, visibility moderate, barometer 1016 millibars. The transport barges Jean Suzon and St. Antoine were hit and sunk by three torpedoes off Cap Roux. The crews were picked up by the support boat. The Cannes MTB unit ran aground whilst hunting the submarine. Mission abandoned at 19.00 hours. No result."
The following note was later added to the log: "Further to the sinking of the Jean Suzon and the St. Antoine, 1 crewman died, 3 were injured and 7 are missing."

Diving to the wreck

The wrecks of the two barges are to be found at depths ranging from 24 to 32 metres, lying on a gently sloping algae-covered sea-bed. What at first sight appear to be the stern, the prow and the centre section of a large vessel are in fact the stern and the after section of the two shattered barges which virtually fused together in the explosion provoked by the torpedoes.
The principal elements of the two vessels are strewn over an area of 100 square metres in this kind of ships' graveyard. Swimming over this area you get an immediate impression of the violence and drama of the explosion: the sea-bed is covered with wreckage from the two barges. The impact with

A - A number of divers, as this exceptional archive photograph documents, descended to the wrecks off Anthéor just a few years after the end of the war. As you can see, the machine-guns were still mounted on their supports.

B - Although the violence of the explosion almost literally disintegrated the two stubby vessels, the stern section of one of them, complete with the rudder, has remained virtually intact.

C - The Jean Suzon and the St. Antoine met their fate on the 31st of January, 1944, when they were sunk by torpedoes launched by the British submarine H.M.S. Untiring.

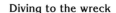

B

C

the torpedoes and the subsequent explosion triggered much of the cargo of munitions carried on board. Not all of the cargo exploded, however, and large calibre shells can be seen stacked in their hundreds in the holds and scattered around the wrecks. They are no longer dangerous as over the course of the years they have corroded and lost their explosive potential.

Your dive begins at the stern, at a depth of 27 metres.

The small propeller is almost intact, but the rudder is bent and damaged against the starboard side of the vessel; you can however, observe the barges' antiquated steering gear consisting of long rods and a wheel.

The stern is heavy and rounded, typical of the barges of that era as well as of more modern versions. The superstructure at the rear is now showing its age: a large section has broken away and is lying on the sea-bed alongside the wreck. It is worth entering the hold through the gaping stern. Illuminating the nooks with your torch you will discover the inhabitants of the wreck: countless moray and conger eels as well as scorpionfish of considerable dimensions.

On the starboard side you will find great quantity of artillery shells which resemble large swollen marrows spilling from the belly of the vessel, or what remains of it. The munitions are now used as hideaways by the moray eels, and it is possible to see two or three of these fish crowding into the same haven. Moving from the starboard side at an angle of 45°, and following the gently sloping sea-bed, you cross a veritable cemetery full of scrap metal. It really is difficult to imagine that at one time this distorted, confused mass of steel scattered across the bottom of the sea was once two separate vessels. Examining the wreckage closely you will be able to identify stretches of rail and a number of trolleys used load and unload the heaviest munitions.

The exploration of the "scrapyard" leads to the second section of the

wreck which lies at a depth of 32 metres. This is the prow of one of the two barges, but it has not been possible to establish whether it is from the *Jean Suzon* or the *St. Antoine*. This forward section is around 8 metres long, and is stubby and constructed without a keel or stempost, an architecture typical of the heavy, slow transport vessels that slide though the water without parting it. The anchor capstan, the bollard, the hawsers and the armour are all still in place.

In order to dive safely you should bear in mind that to explore both sections of the Anthéor barges you are obliged to swim for some distance: you have to leave from your cover boat's anchor, cover the whole area and return to your starting point.

If your cover boat follows your air bubbles you can be picked up in the open sea, naturally after having completed a decompression stop.

The dive is not affected by currents as in this area they are rarely strong.

D

E

F

D - The large rectangular rudder of one of the two barges, although partially unhinged by the impact with the sea-bed, is still in place.

E - In the right-hand side of this photo you can see the metal structure which once supported the missing ship's wheel.

F - A diver hovering just over part of one of the barge's fairly antiquated steering gear.

THE B-17 OF CALVI
by Andrea Ghisotti

RATINGS

Location difficulty: average.
Visibility: good.
Currents: scarce.
Diving difficulty: scarce.
Lines or nets: none.
Historical interest: high.
Photographic interest: high.
Biological interest: scarce.

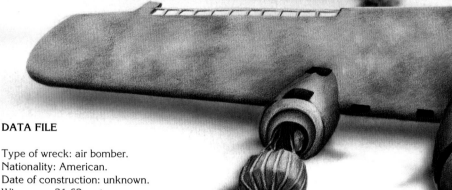

DATA FILE

Type of wreck: air bomber.
Nationality: American.
Date of construction: unknown.
Wingspan: 31.62 metres.
Length: 22.66 metres.
Weight at take off: 29,710 kilos.
Date of crash: 2.14.1944.
Cause of crash: damage by enemy
         fighters.
Localisation: in front of the
         Calvi Citadel.
Distance from the shore: 200 metres.
Minimum depth: 23 metres.
Maximum depth: 27 metres.

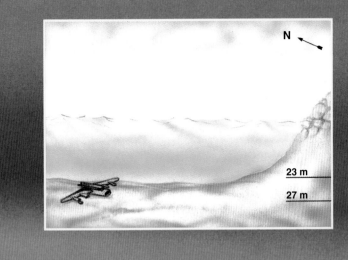

23 m

27 m

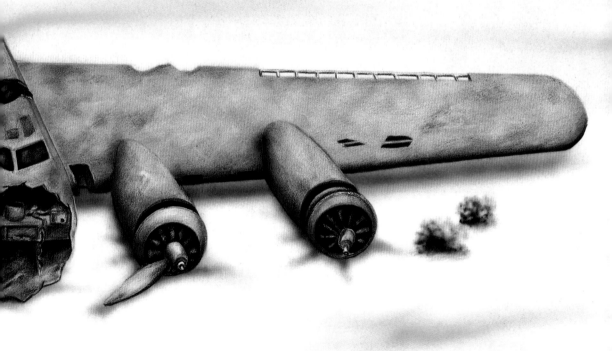

For years the history of this great Flying Fortress remained unknown, and the official version of the facts appeared to be that of Paul Valeani, the "father" of this aircraft, who ran a diving centre at Calvi during the Sixties. Valeani was the first to take an interest in the story and he dedicated dozens and dozens of dives to a reconstruction of the facts.

It was one of his articles, published by a local paper, which triggered the official enquiries. Among the 5,000 American aircraft lost over the Mediterranean, there was no record of this particular B-17, and so an American expert stationed in Germany was sent to Calvi and asked Valeani to search for clues and traces among the wreckage.

The diver eventually came across a wallet containing a stainless steel dog-tag generally worn around the aviators' necks which allowed the true story to be reconstructed.

It should be pointed out that Valeani's version of the facts was very close to the events that actually happened, but he dated the crash at around late summer, 1943, a few months earlier than the true date.

The Flying Fortress was a B-17G, serial number 4231044, based in southern Italy. She took off on her last mission on the 14th of February, 1944 under the command of Frank Chaplick. The plane was taking part in one of the carpet bombing missions which involved dozens of Flying Fortresses escorted by squadrons of fighters.

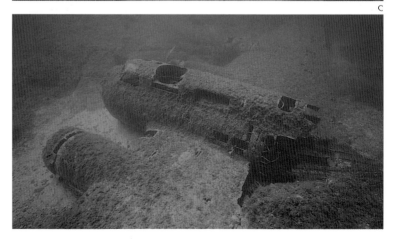

A - The B-17 was the most famous American bomber of the Second World War. The model G produced form 1943, was the last to leave the Boeing assembly lines. During the Second World War was produced a total of 12,731 B-17 Flying Fortresses.

B - The wreck of the B-17 is lying in front of the port of Calvi in Corsica, at a depth of around 25 metres. The Flying Fortress is still in good condition and, thanks above all to its wingspan of over 30 metres, provides a remarkable spectacle.

C - The B-17 is symbolic of the might of the American war machine. The model G in particular had a weight at take-off of almost 30 tonnes, was defended by 13 machine-guns, could carry a little under 8 tonnes of bombs and had a range of 3,220 kilometres.

Whilst the bombers were approaching the target a correction was made to the flight path and "our" B-17, on the outside of the formation, was left isolated. It was immediately attacked by the enemy fighters which knocked out one of the engines and damaged the superchargers of two others. The Flying Fortresses were renowned for their durability and strength and were capable of absorbing quite incredible damage and still carry on flying. That first attack was terrible, however, the radio operator and the left-hand forward gunner had been killed, the upper turret had been put out of commission, the lower turret gunner was slightly injured, the tail gunner more seriously and the oxygen masks of the pilot and the navigator were unusable.

The plane was thus in no condition to defend itself, and robust as it was, it could not have resisted the attacks of the fighters for much longer. When the tail gunner informed the pilot that his strength was fading fast the captain decided to dump the bomb load. This was done just in time as immediately afterwards the fuselage was penetrated by a 20 mm cannon shell which would probably have detonated the entire load and consequently destroyed the aircraft.

The enemy fighters finally decided to abandon their prey and the B-17 was briefly escorted by three P 47's.

A return to base was out of the question given the plane's condition. A route was consequently plotted to Corsica, with the plane gradually losing height as it crossed the Mediterranean.

The airfield at Calvi was finally sighted but the runway was very short for a Flying Fortress and was also surrounded by mountains.

Having received authorisation, Chaplick made an initial, unsuccessful attempt to put the plane down but was forced to head back out to sea.

By this time only the right-hand

D

E

F

D - In this view you can see the round hole just behind the cockpit in which the upper turret was once housed. This mechanically operated unit was armed with two 12.7 mm machine-guns.

E - Although the glazed nose of the bomber was destroyed when she hit the waves, the cabin is fairly intact. A couple of windows even still have their glass.

F - A diver hovering over the upper turret housing; around the inner perimeter you can still see toothed ring which allowed it to rotate.

inner engine was working, and even for a muscular 1,200 hp Wright-Cyclone, 27,000 kilos of Flying Fortress were a little too much too bear.

The massive, insurmountable bulk of the citadel appeared in front of the plane, but the pilot had already decided to ditch his aircraft. Around 500-700 metres before the point of impact the remaining ammunition, around a tonne, was dumped.

As the plane touched the waves Chaplick pulled her nose up to as to slow her progress with the tail and succeeded in putting the huge machine down onto the water, losing the tailplane in the process. The aircraft remained afloat for a total of two minutes, long enough for the six survivors to scramble out of the fuselage and throw the self-inflating life-rafts into the water.

The crew's adventure ended soon afterwards when they were picked up by the British Air Sea Rescue. The Flying Fortress had in the meantime disappeared, sliding down to lie on the bottom at a depth of 25 metres, on a field of sea grass amongst the rocks and isolated masses.

The bodies of the three dead crew members went down with her. When Paul Valeani dived in the Sixties the aircraft was still in an excellent state of preservation and nothing had been touched.

There were still two machine guns in perfect working order, one at the front and one at the rear. Numerous parachutes (more than the number of crew members) were also found, together with oxygen tanks and the remains of the dead airmen.

Diving to the wreck

Fifty years after it slipped beneath the waves, the Calvi Flying Fortress remains one of the most exciting dives to an aircraft wreck thanks to the favourable environmental conditions and the generally intact condition of the plane. It is not a difficult dive and the greatest danger concerns the constant coming and going of boats of every type during the

A

B

C

A - The B-17G was powered by four air-cooled Wright R-1820-97 Cyclone engines with nine radial cylinders, with each unit producing 1,200 hp. At maximum power, these engines provided the heavy bomber with a top speed of 462 kph.

B - The bomb aimer, responsible for releasing the bombs, and the forward gunner were housed in the nose section which is missing from the Calvi B-17.

C - In this shot you can easily see the large retractable tail-wheel ripped from its housing in the fuselage when the plane was ditched.

summer months, the wreck lying on the approach route for those reaching Calvi from the South. The most stunning visual impact is gained by diving slightly closer to the shore moving in the same direction as the plane.

The great bird, with its fully spread wings, can be seen after just a few metres descent and is a truly stirring sight.

The B-17 had a wingspan of no less than 31.6 metres and in this case the wings are intact.

This is by no means common given that an aircraft structure is much more fragile than that of a ship.

As you move closer you will notice the four engines, all still present although the first on the right (on the left from the front) has fallen to the sandy bottom. Most of the propeller blades have unfortunately been removed. Only one blade attached to the inner left-hand engine and three from the inner right-hand unit remain. The first photos taken in the Sixties allow a deduction to be made. The missing blades were straight, whilst those of the inner right-hand engine are bent. This usually happens when a plane ditches with a propeller under power, and thus the only engine still working was the inner right which still retains its propeller.

As I said, the wings are impressively large with rounded tips. You can still see the lights on the leading edges, faired in with Plexiglas.

The nose of the aircraft was destroyed during the crash landing and when it hit the bottom. You can now see a tangle of wires, batteries and cables.

The cockpit is in good condition and particularly evocative with its two metal seats and various controls between them.

One of the glass panels in the roof is still in place, the other has disappeared. Behind the cockpit there is a circular aperture, that of the upper turret. The cupola and the gun have both disappeared but the "perch" is still there.

A few metres further back the fuselage has been sliced open allowing you to see and, with due caution, move inside. The encrustations covering the entire structure are fantastic. Among the wreckage on the sea bottom you can still find the incredibly durable remains of the parachutes which have survived 50 years immersion in salt water. Moving out to sea (here we are at a depth of 27 metres) you can see the remains of the tail some distance away and, on the left, those of the tail-wheel with its tyre still in place.

Lastly, do not forget to look under the wings where a huge conger has made its lair and where small lobsters are also a common sight.

D

D - The inner-right engine is the only one to still feature all three dural propeller blades: the fact that they are bent backwards suggests that this must have been the only engine still functioning when the plane hit the water.

E

E - A diver observing the large landing light installed in the leading edge of the left-hand wing: note that the Plexiglas fairing is undamaged.

F - When ditching their aircraft, pilots had to pull the nose up at the last moment so that the tail touched the water first and softened the bow somewhat. This explains why the Calvi B-17's fuselage is truncated at its mid-point.

F

G - The interior of the cockpit still features some of the original instrumentation and the pilot and co-pilot's seat one beside the other; in front of them in this shot you can see the throttle levers for the four engines.

G

THE VICKERS VIKING OF MORTOLI
by Andrea Ghisotti

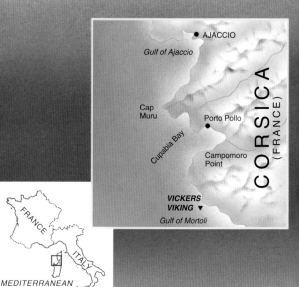

RATINGS

Location difficulty: average.
Visibility: excellent.
Currents: scarce.
Diving difficulty: scarce.
Lines and nets: none.
Historical interest: average.
Photographic interest: high.
Biological interest: average.

DATA FILE

Type of wreck: air carrier.
Nationality: British.
Date of construction: unknown.
Wingspan: 27.12 metres.
Length: 19.86 metres.
Weight at take off: 15,422 kilos.
Date of crash: unknown.
Cause of crash: engine failure.
Geographical co-ordinates:
      41°31'21" N, 8°52'21" E
Localisation: 256° Latoniccia Island,
      149° Mortoli Point.
Distance from shore: 200 metres.
Minimum depth: 11 metres.
Maximum depth: 13 metres.

11 m

13 m

N

A

A - The Vickers Viking, *introduced early in 1946, was one of the most successful mid-range civil transport planes produced by the British aircraft industry in the years immediately following the war. One hundred and sixty-one examples were built and were used intensively until the mid-Fifties.*

During the 1950's a *Vickers Viking* flew over southern Corsica with an exceptional group of passengers: the famous Holiday on Ice skaters. The plane was a twin-engine 491 Viking, built by the British manufacturer Vickers Armstrong Ltd. from 1946, and closely related to the Wellington bomber which had served with great honour during the Second World War.
In the cabin the unmistakable drone of the two 1,690 hp Bristol Hercules 634 radial engines could clearly be heard; music to the ears of aircraft enthusiasts.
These very engines were the cause of the problems which afflicted this particular *Vikers Viking*.
As the plane lost height the pilot had to find a suitable site for an emergency landing in a hurry.
The long beach at Mortoli appeared to provide the answer, and the pilot took the plane down until it was brushing the sand.
To his horror he realised that there were rocks mid-way along the beach and that the remaining portion was far too short and ended in cliffs against which he would crash.
Given the condition of the engines there was no question of climbing again and so he headed straight out to sea, deciding to ditch.
He quickly raised the undercarriage and as the fuselage was kissing the tops of the waves, pulled up the nose to slow the plane's progress with the tail.

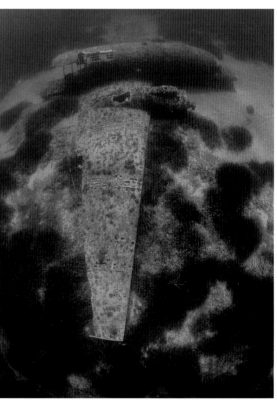

B

B - Like an immense surreal bird with out-spread wings, the Vickers Viking *is lying on sand in front of the beach at Mortoli at a depth of just 13 metres. The photograph reveals the wingspan of over 27 metres.*

The manoeuvre was executed perfectly, although the tail section was destroyed in the process. The fuselage remained afloat long enough, however, for all the members of the troupe and the crew to dive into the sea and swim to the nearby shore.

The plane sank, but given that the water was shallow did not have far to travel. She came to rest amidst white sand and sea grass at a depth of just 13 metres. When there are no victims the news of an accident tends to attract little interest, and in this case there was just the odd paragraph in the daily papers, mainly due to the fame of the troupe, and then the incident was virtually forgotten. In the meantime the wreck began to be colonised by the local flora and fauna which were only too happy to find a new habitat in the middle of the sandy sea-bed.

During the next decade divers began to frequent the wreck, unfortunately sawing through and taking away the propeller blades. The wreck has otherwise remained virtually intact, however, and was used as the setting for an excellent short film entitled *Mare Nostrum*.

Diving to the wreck

It is not easy to localise the exact site of the aircraft as it does not correspond to the position described by Joncheray in his beautiful wreck books.
During the summer months, however, it is by no means

C

C - The cabin of the plane has survived the violence of the ditching virtually unscathed; the Viking usually carried a crew of five.

D

E

D - The Vickers Viking *could transport 24/36 passengers depending on the internal conformation and the length of the flight, with a maximum range of 2,735 kilometres.*

E - At the point where the wing meets the fuselage, close to the leading edge, the metal skin has come adrift, exposing the unusual geodesic structure derived from that of the famous Wellington bomber.

tail section is hidden, the *Vickers Viking* really does appear intact. You can make a very detailed, leisurely inspection of the wreck given the insignificant depth at which it is lying and the restricted area. There is slight damage to the nose on the right-hand side, perhaps caused by the impact with the sea-bed.

The wings are intact, with the two very interesting radial engines in place, albeit shorn of their propellers.

The aerodynamic cowlings over the engines continue towards the rear, forming the undercarriage bays. You can still clearly see the single large tyre housed in each wing.

You can inspect the interior of the fuselage through the long line of windows, although it is better to go straight to the point at the rear where the tail has been sharply truncated. Access to the interior from here is easy, especially as the seats which would have hampered your movements have disappeared.

A - A diver is hovering over the large starboard engine. During its long career, the Viking *became the first British commercial aircraft to be powered by jet engines. In 1948 an example was specially modified to accept two Rolls-Royce Nene jets.*

B - The Vickers Viking *was powered by two 14-cylinder, air-cooled, Bristol Hercules 634 radial engines, each producing 1,690 hp. They provided the aircraft with a cruising speed of 338 kph.*

uncommon to find divers' boats anchored over the site as it is well known among the habitués of the beach at Mortoli.

It is a very easy dive.

The autonomy provided by breathing gear naturally allows you to explore all its secrets and even the interior of the plane.

I have only one particular piece of advice: do not anchor directly over the wreck.

Unfortunately I was an eye witness to an incident in which a sailing boat had caught its anchor in the structure and ripped away a large piece of the metal skin whilst trying to pull it up.

The clarity of the water is incredible and on certain days you can see the wreck when standing on the deck of your cover boat without even having to put your head in the water.

The sight is even more suggestive floating in front of the nose of the aircraft as you get the impression that it is flying towards you.

The wingspan is considerable, 27.20 metres to be precise, and from a certain angle at which the

C - The interior of the spacious fuselage is now completely bare; the seats and all other furnishing elements have disappeared and you can thus swim easily up to the cockpit.

D, E - Like the cabin, the cockpit is almost completely empty. The seats and much of the instrumentation was removed long ago by the usual souvenir hunters.

F - The gondola of the left-hand motor has been partially uncovered, and through the aperture you can see the large tyre fitted to the undercarriage.

D

E

The fuselage is thus a long empty tunnel rendered interesting by the encrustations of sponges, bryozoa, sea-squirts and annelids which enliven the monochrome aluminium panelling.
There are also many fish which have taken up residence in the plane.
Moving without stirring up the sediment with your fins you reach the cockpit.
It is well illuminated thanks to the large windows, and the tangles of wiring hanging everywhere create a certain impression.
The instrumentation has been removed, as have the seats, but the space is still very evocative.
Enthusiasts will be able to discover for themselves the myriad tiny details which only a careful and expert eye will notice, although the encrustations have by now obliterated the data which would have allowed us to identify the aircraft precisely.

F

THE CANADAIR CL215 OF SAGONE
by Andrea Ghisotti

CORSICA (FRANCE)

Gulf of Porto

Cap Rossu

CARGÈSE

SAGONE

CANADAIR

Gulf of Sagone

FRANCE

ITALY

MEDITERRANEAN SEA

RATINGS

Location difficulty: high.
Visibility: excellent.
Currents: scarce.
Diving difficulty: average.
Lines or nets: none.
Historical interest: low.
Photographic interest: average.
Biological interest: low.

DATA FILE

Type of wreck: curcraft
Nationality: French.
Date of construction: unknown.
Wingspan: 28.60 metres.
Length: 19.82 metres.
Weight at take off: 19,731 kilos.
Date of crash: 9.3.1971.
Cause of crash: damage to fuselage.
Geographical co-ordinates:
     42°06'07" N, 8°41'13" E.
Localisation: 8° Sagone tower,
     273° Triu Point.
Distance from shore: 200 metres.
Minimum depth: 29 metres.
Maximum depth: 32 metres.

29 m

32 m

N

THE CANADAIR CL215

The forest fire plague which each year destroys much of the Mediterranean woodlands is well known, and during the summer months the newspapers are unfortunately full of reports on the phenomenon.

The most efficient means of dealing with the flames are the fire-fighting planes which many

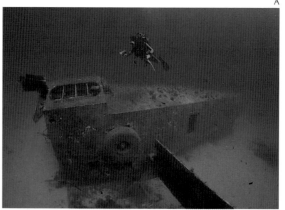

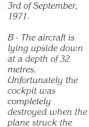

A

A - A diver is examining the rear section of the Canadair *which crashed in the Gulf of Sagone on the 3rd of September, 1971.*

B - The aircraft is lying upside down at a depth of 32 metres. Unfortunately the cockpit was completely destroyed when the plane struck the bottom nose-first.

B

C

of us have seen in operation, if only on the television.

The aircraft used for this purpose throughout the Mediterranean basin and in many other countries is the *CL215*, built at Montreal by the aircraft manufacturer Canadair, the name usually adopted to identify the model. The *CL215* made its maiden flight on the 23rd of October, 1967, and it soon gained a universal reputation for its robustness and efficiency. The fuselage is watertight and buoyant, and is kept in horizontal trim by two wing-tip floats.

The undercarriage can be partially retracted into the fuselage and allows the plane to touch down on dry land too, making it a true amphibian. The *Canadair* is fitted with two eighteen-cylinder Double Wasp CA3 radial engines built by Pratt and Whitney which

provide it with a take-off power of 2,100 hp. It is equipped with two water tanks providing a total capacity of 5,346 litres which are filled in a few seconds whilst the plane is on the water. Those who have watched the fire-fighting operations will have noted the rapidity with which the tanks are filled compared with the slowness of the flight: it takes moments to refill the tanks and ages to get the water to the site of the fire and return to refill once again. Nevertheless, a single aircraft can perform as many as 200 sea-fire trips in a day and we all owe a great deal to these planes which, over their twenty-five-year career, have saved much of our woodland heritage. The story of the *Canadair* at Sagone began like many other summer alarms: a fire had broken out on the hills surrounding the Gulf of Sagone,

to the North of Ajaccio on the 2nd of September, 1971. The fire proved difficult to extinguish and the following morning the help of the civil guard was requested with two Canadairs immediately being despatched. One of these, registration number F-Z BBG, serial number 1025, named *Pelican 25*, commanded by Jean-Paul Patillaud, returned to the bay to refill its tanks after having jettisoned its first load over the flames. Whilst the pilot was concentrating on the delicate manoeuvre of planing across the water, keeping the aircraft horizontal, the co-pilot Jacques Lebel operated the device which allowed the tanks to be refilled. Suddenly the aircraft braked brusquely, the nose diving below the water and the tail rising into the air. Shocked but unhurt, the two pilots succeeded in scrambling out of the cockpit and dived into the sea where they were rescued by a passing boat.

The aircraft in the meantime maintained its upright position and remained afloat for some time, allowing the launch Saint-Appien of the Gendarmerie Maritime to arrive and note a long gash in the watertight underbelly of the Canadair.

The plane eventually sank to the sea-bed where it settled upside down at a depth of 32 metres, damaging its nose during the impact. Subsequently the engines and much of the equipment were salvaged and then the plane was left in peace.

The cause of the crash was

probably a defect in one of the water loading chutes which transferred stress to the airframe, provoking the damage to the fuselage.

Diving to the wreck

It is not easy to locate the *Canadair* lying around 200 metres off the Northern coast of the bay, some distance from the sandy beach crowning the Eastern side. It is worthwhile going directly to the Club Subaquatique de Sagone based at the Cyrnos Hotel which organises accompanied visits to the wreck. The dive itself is easy given that the flat, sandy bottom lies at a depth of 32 metres, and that the water is very clear and allows the wreck to be spotted after descending just a few metres. As you descend the vague shape becomes gradually more distinct until you can clearly see the inverted fuselage and the tail buried sand. As is always the case with fairly small wrecks, it is worth moving over the entire area in open water before descending to the bottom. This allows you to get a much better idea of the overall structure and to take good panoramic photos before the sediment is disturbed by close-up examination.
The front part of the plane was destroyed so you immediately come across the section housing the water tanks.
One of the loading chutes, probably the one responsible for the crash, is missing, whilst the other is closed. It is easy to enter the fuselage from the front, but the structure is empty except for the attractive encrustations.
The undercarriage is very interesting, with two large tyres carrying metal plates with details of the manufacturer.
The tail is intact but well buried in the sand, whilst the wings are in good condition, albeit missing the engines, and they still carry their air force markings.
A beautiful grouper *(Epinephelus alexandrinus)* has made its home beneath one of the wings and pays little attention to divers.

D

E

F

G

C - The Canadair was designed so that the two water tanks could be filled extremly rapidly. In just a few seconds the plane is capable of taking on no less than 5,346 litres of water. This photograph clearly shows the tanks, with the right-hand one lacking its hatch.

D - The metalwork at the front of the aircraft is dramatically torn and distorted.

E - A diver illuminating the markings of the Pelican 25, registration number F-Z BBG, still visible on the wings.

F - It is always exciting to enter a wreck. This photograph shows the virtually empty fuselage which has already been invaded by sand.

G - A diver exploring the interior of the Canadair. Little remains inside the wreck, and the engines and any other components that could be recovered were salvaged following the crash. This shot illustrates the forward section of the plane, partially occupied by the water tanks.

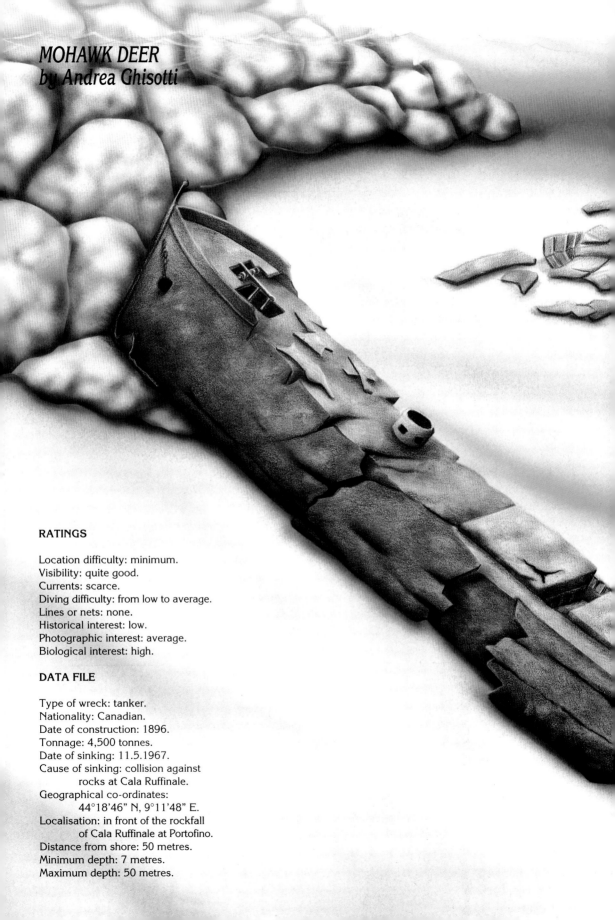

MOHAWK DEER
by Andrea Ghisotti

RATINGS

Location difficulty: minimum.
Visibility: quite good.
Currents: scarce.
Diving difficulty: from low to average.
Lines or nets: none.
Historical interest: low.
Photographic interest: average.
Biological interest: high.

DATA FILE

Type of wreck: tanker.
Nationality: Canadian.
Date of construction: 1896.
Tonnage: 4,500 tonnes.
Date of sinking: 11.5.1967.
Cause of sinking: collision against
          rocks at Cala Ruffinale.
Geographical co-ordinates:
          44°18'46" N, 9°11'48" E.
Localisation: in front of the rockfall
          of Cala Ruffinale at Portofino.
Distance from shore: 50 metres.
Minimum depth: 7 metres.
Maximum depth: 50 metres.

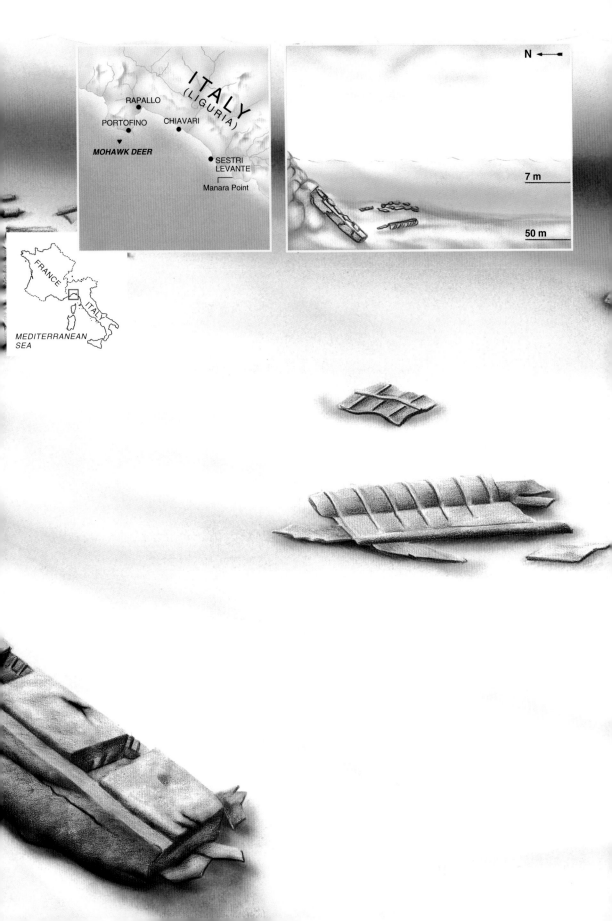

ITALY
(LIGURIA)

RAPALLO

PORTOFINO   CHIAVARI

MOHAWK DEER

SESTRI
LEVANTE

Manara Point

FRANCE

ITALY

MEDITERRANEAN
SEA

N

7 m

50 m

THE MOHAWK DEER

Mohawk Deer was an odd name for what was a rather unattractive ship, an old Canadian tanker of 4,500 tonnes launched at West Bay City way back in 1896 and registered at Montreal.

Following a long, but anonymous career, for one obscure motive or another the *Mohawk Deer* found herself on the other side of the ocean destined for the cutting flames of a scrapping yard at La Spezia. This was in the November of 1967, and her final voyage out of the port of Genoa, with the ship already stripped bare, was entrusted to the towing power of the Yugoslav tug *Yunak*.

The weather conditions were poor however, the libeccio was blowing and the forecasts predicted that it would intensify over the next few hours. The Captain of the *Yunak* nevertheless insisted on leaving with a double tow, the *Mohawk Deer* and the *Makawell*, a 2,600-tonne ship. Off the Portofino Promontory the sea conditions were already prohibitive, and the strain on the towing lines was enough to snap the robust steel cable and set the *Mohawk Deer* adrift. There was no way of recovering the ship with the swell that was running and with a second ship in tow, and the Captain of the *Yunak* radioed to Genoa for assistance.

It was November 5th, a Sunday, and the fact that there was nobody aboard the ship slowed up the rescue operations.

There were the usual negotiations between the salvage vessels and the insurance company over the cost of the operation, and by the time two tugs eventually arrived from Genoa it was too late.

The waves had pushed the ship ashore onto the part of the Promontory known as Cala Ruffinale or Cala degli Inglesi. There was nothing to be done except to bear witness to the ship's final agonies as it was battered against the rocks. She eventually broke in two stern-

side of amidships and was literally pounded by the waves.

There was initially talk of salvaging what remained of the ship, but the cost of the operation would have been greater than the scrap value of the metal, estimated at around forty thousand pounds. She was consequently left in peace and ever since has formed an integral part of the undersea panorama of the Promontory. As soon as the sea was calmer divers began visiting the wreck, but there was little worth recovering: the navigation lights, the odd piece of equipment but not much else. At that time the foremast could still be seen standing proud above the waves and remained that way for some months before sinking just below the surface.

The stern section was easily located given that a considerable area of rock had been incised by blows dealt by the wreck, and the niches were filled with fragments of metal which even today, thirty years on, continue to bleed rust and confer a reddish-brown hue to the point of impact. The two sections of the wreck lie around a hundred metres apart, the bow further to the West towards the centre of the bay, the stern towards the East. Divers from all over could not have asked for a better present; the wreck is in fact perfect for submarine exploration.

A, B - These newspapers dating from the era of the sinking, illustrate the last moments of the Canadian tanker with dramatic photographs.

C - In order to fully explore the two sections of the Mohawk Deer you need to make at least two dives - three if you also want to look into the holds.

The dive begins in shallow water and is therefore ideal for beginners, but also goes on to reach considerable depths.
It is a large wreck, with an impressive, evocative bow and is fully accessible with its empty holds which fortunately have not been responsible for any pollution. Lastly, the sea bottom in that area was not particularly exciting, a pebbled bed with a few scattered rocks leading out to sea.
The wreck has provided an extremely interesting focal point and is now visited by thousands of divers each year, making it one of the most popular in the Mediterranean.

Diving to the wreck

At least two dives are need to explore the *Mohawk Deer*, three if you want to see the boilers too, although this is a dive reserved for experts only. The bow section is the most intact and attractive, especially if you dive from the shore, heading out to sea until you see the dead-straight vertical prow typical of the ships of the turn of the century.
It is a breathtaking sight, especially if it is your first wreck. The highest point, a short flag standard welded to the prow is at a depth of sixteen metres. It is better to descend along the exterior, exploring the two large hawse-holes, the one to port lacks its anchor, but the chain is still there. The movement of the water has caused the chain to swing to and fro, wearing away the plating. The starboard anchor was still in place until a few years ago until some "Rambo of the depths" sawed through the chain, leaving it to fall to the bottom. It can still be seen there, and hopefully there it will remain.
It is worth descending to the bottom, a depth of 23 metres, to see the point of impact between the prow and the rocks.
The steel cutwater, a good 12 centimetres thick, is as bent and crumpled as if it were made of cardboard. Moving into open water you gain a clear sight of the forecastle with massive capstans

D

E

F

G

D - The imposing prow of the Mohawk Deer stands out sharply against the blue surface of the sea.

E - This mass of distorted scrap metal is what remains of the stern section following the dramatic incident of the 5th of November, 1967.

F - On the lower deck you can see a large capstan, home to the extraordinary organisms typical of the Ligurian promontory.

G - There are also large capstans below the quarterdeck. In this shot a lobster is emerging from the encrusted equipment.

set below deck-level, an unusual arrangement.
Do not miss visiting the lower deck. Alongside the capstan there is a large bollard with the severed towing cable responsible for the wreck still wrapped around it. Further below there are the anchor bays, but this area is a tight fit and not recommended for those suffering from claustrophobia. Keeping to the centre of the deck and descending to round 30 metres, you can see an inverted semi-circular structure which was once perhaps the bridge, and which once carried the mast. This section was transformed during the winter of 1973 following a structural collapse. The exploration

continues along the left-hand side (the starboard flank of the ship), where the deck has folded over on itself to form a kind of long corridor regularly interrupted by large apertures.

This area allows you to enjoy the thrill of exploring the interior of a wreck with the reassuring light of the next aperture always in sight. The roof of these false holds is incredibly encrusted with yellow madrepores *(Leptosammia pruvoti)* in the midst of which, years ago, I discovered branches of red coral which had rooted perfectly on the plating.

Together with the late Doctor Giorgio Barletta, then the director of the Milan Civic Aquarium,

B

A

C

D

A - The tanker's starboard anchor is still present. Unfortunately some vandal has cut through the chain, undoubtedly in an attempt to carry it away.

B - The exploration of the interior of the Mohawk Deer is reserved for expert divers only. It offers the opportunity to admire some beautiful gorgonians.

C - One of the greatest diving thrills is when you come across elements that revive a wreck. This photograph shows one of the bollards on the forecastle with the remains of the towing cable still wrapped around it.

D - The capstan at the prow also evokes the frenetic activity which took place on the ship from way back in 1896, the year in which she was launched at West Bay City.

100

we organised a programme to measure the branches given that it was one of the first cases in which the coral could be precisely dated, a factor indispensable in studying growth rates.

Then as often happens the coral branches were in part pillaged by some underwater adventurer. The *Mohawk Deer* is still, however, an extremely rich and interesting biological laboratory. For example, it houses all five of the most common species of Mediterranean sea fans and examples of almost all the organisms present on the Promontory.

The exploration of the bow section finishes at a depth of around 43-44 metres where the plates were torn apart by the violence of the sea. The stern section is lying in shallower waters (at depths between 7 and 25 metres), although some elements have rolled further down and provide material for an interesting second dive. This section is unfairly snubbed by some divers, but it is actually a hair-raising illustration of the power of the sea. There is, in fact, no longer any trace of the ship as it once was, and you move over a mass of plates, girders and metal scrap which appear to be the result of some explosion. Careful examination of the wreckage reveals many interesting details. The rudder, for example, has been thrown into the middle of wreckage forward of the engine room. The connecting rods and the massive crankshaft of the engines can be recognised, whilst further eastwards lies a capstan and, in deeper water, the remains of the quarterdeck. This leaves the deepest dive, for experts accompanied by a guide. Descending at the correct point and heading out to sea, at a depth of 50 metres you find the two huge boilers lying on the muddy bottom, ancient heat exchangers from the last century which have scattered pieces of coal across the sea-bed and which are inhabited by schools of Anthias *(Pseudanthias squamipinnis)*, a fabulous sight when the water is clear.

E

F

G

H

E - This photograph shows the chains leading from the capstans to the hawse-holes.

F - The large "windows" of the small semi-circular bridge look out into the infinite blue. Access to this area of the ship is not particularly difficult and offers continual surprises and emotions.

G - The Mohawk Deer did not have a particularly remarkable career, and is probably better appreciated now as a wreck, with gorgonians, madrepores and bryozoas flourishing on her plates.

H - The plates of the forward section are encrusted with organisms and multi-coloured gorgonians. The wreck is a veritable biological laboratory in which all the five principal species of Mediterranean gorgonians can be found.

GENOVA
by Andrea Ghisotti

RATINGS

Location difficulty: average.
Visibility: scarce.
Currents: scarce.
Diving difficulty: high.
Lines and nets: many.
Historical interest: high.
Photographic interest: average.
Biological interest: average.

DATA FILE

Type of wreck: merchant ship.
Nationality: Italian.
Date of construction: 1904.
Tonnage: 3,486 tonnes.
Date of sinking: 7.27.1917.
Cause of sinking: torpedo.
Geographical co-ordinates:
    44°18'52" N, 9°13'47" E.
Localisation: 279° Paraggi Castle,
    201° Portofino Point.
Distance from shore: 900 metres.
Minimum depth: 45 metres.
Maximum depth: 61 metres.

THE GENOVA

It was a warm day in late July, 1917. The First World War was at its peak and many ships had already been sent to the bottom of the Mediterranean.

The *Genova* was an attractive steamship of 3,486 tonnes gross, 2,220 net, with a deadweight capacity of 6,750 tonnes, owned by Ilva of Rome and built in 1904. On the 27th of July it was transporting an important cargo of cannons and other war materials, but it had no escort to protect it from the insidious enemy submarines. It was thus child's play for the crew of a German U-boat to launch the torpedo which struck her on the starboard side in correspondence with the first bow hold.

The large steamer did not sink at once, however. She managed to limp as far as the bay of Paraggi where she anchored below the castle and the entire crew was taken off unhurt.

The ship's final agonies were prolonged - lasting no less than 8 hours according to contemporary reports.

She finally went down bow first, and settled perfectly upright at a depth of 60 metres just out of the bay. An enquiry was opened as it was inconceivable that in eight hours nobody had thought to tow her to Santa Margherita or Rapallo where the cargo and perhaps the ship may have been saved.

After the war a Genoese salvage firm worked on the wreck, with the divers succeeding in opening the holds and recovering the entire cargo. The ship was then largely forgotten and only the fishermen lowered their lines over what they called *Il Vapore*.

When I rediscovered her underwater there were few who remembered her. I had gathered information among the sailors and fishermen of Portofino and they were all agreed that I would find nothing more than a few rusting plates. It was quite a shock when, after a dive into the green depths,

I reached the turbid mud of the bottom at 60 metres, swam in the probable direction of the wreck and suddenly found myself in front of a wall as high as a three-storey house! The colossal *Genova* was anything but destroyed; in spite of almost eighty years spent at the bottom of the Mediterranean she was still in excellent condition.

Diving to the wreck

This is a very demanding dive and should only be undertaken by expert divers with experience of deep wrecks. It should also only be made in summer in excellent sea conditions, and with perfect underwater and surface organization.

The wreck is located in the middle of the Gulf on a route used by boats and ferries, and lies on bed of very fine mud.

The slightest sea-bed current will stir this mud into suspension, drastically reducing visibility.

The wreck is completely entwined with nets, lines and abandoned anchor ropes, and it would be extremely dangerous to be trapped in this web in the conditions of poor visibility which may occur even during the summer. It is therefore obligatory to descend following a weighted line lowered over the centre of the ship. The wreck is around a hundred metres long and you will need at least two dives to explore

A - A diver illuminating the nets which are wrapped round the starboard wing of the Genova's bridge. The Italian ship was built in 1904 and sank at the end of July, 1917.

B - At the rear of the central superstructure, you can still see the remains of the funnel, once impressive but now almost completely destroyed, and the ventilator ducts.

C - The exploration of the Genova is undoubtedly exciting but you should always bear in mind that as she is lying at a depth of over 50 metres, the dive is suitable for experts only. The photograph portrays the forecastle with a capstan in the foreground.

a floor to support it.

The flying bridges are very suggestive with their drapery of lines and nets, and stairs leading down to the deck. Here you will find the accessible holds, but they contain nothing more interesting than mud.

After a fair swim (beware depth drunkenness - at this point we are at a depth of 52-53 metres) you reach the forecastle with its full complement of capstans, bollards, hand-rails and other equipment. It terminates in the proud, vertical bow. It is not worth compromising the dive by descending to the bottom which here lies at over 60 metres. The gash provoked by the torpedo is also impressive, with the plates curiously forced outwards.

The exploration of the stern requires a second dive.

The route is almost a mirror image of the first dive to the bow, with the open holds, the very wide deck and masses of lines and ropes everywhere. Beware of a large and robust trawl net which is

wrapped around the stern. This section is very attractive and it is with some surprise that you note that the salvage divers left the large three-bladed propeller in place. Together with the rudder, this element comprises a particularly spectacular sight, all the more so given that both are covered with oysters as is the rest of the stern.

I have to end this description by drawing your attention to the question of safety once again. I was unsure whether to include this wreck in the book, thinking that it was too deep and too dangerous.

Today, however, the wreck is becoming famous and more divers are visiting it.

Better they should do so, therefore, with some knowledge of the structure and the possible dangers.

But bear in mind that although I know it well, and even after dozens of visits, I often postpone diving to the Genova if conditions are not perfect.

D

it all. The best descent route is towards the central quarterdeck which boasts the highest structures comprising the funnel surrounded by a series of black holes which were once ducts leading from the ventilators. The funnel is still impressive, but unfortunately it is beginning to show its age and has partially crumbled.

Below the funnel is the boiler and the engine room, but you should avoid wasting time and move on towards the bow. You thus reach the forward section of the quarterdeck with the remains of the bridge and the cabins where, on the starboard side, you can see a bath tub suspended where once there was

E

F

D - The nets shrouding the starboard wing of the bridge represent a potential danger for divers. In the centre of the photograph you can see the steps leading to the deck.

E - There are some beautiful sponges growing on the forecastle which accentuate the drama of diving to this wreck.

F - Many divers now visit the Genova. Here a group of divers is examining the prow, with its wreckage-strewn deck.

THE KT OF SESTRI
by Andrea Ghisotti

RATINGS

Location difficulty: high.
Visibility: from good to excellent.
Currents: from scarce to average.
Diving difficulty: high.
Lines and nets: many.
Historical interest: high.
Photographic interest: high.
Biological interest: high.

DATA FILE

Type of wreck: minesweeper.
Nationality: German .
Date of construction: unknown.
Tonnage: 600/800 tonnes (aprox.)
Date of sinking: February 1944.
Cause of sinking: torpedo.
Geographical coordinates:
        44°15'76" N, 9°22'02" E.
Localization: 113° P.ta Manara,
        70° Sestri Levante beacon.
Distance from shore: about 1 mile.
Minimum depth: 35 metres.
Maximum depth: 60 metres.

THE KT OF SESTRI

This ship is universally known by the name *KT*, initials perhaps deriving from the German word "Korvette". What is certain is that she was a small vessel, perhaps a minesweeper or a corvette, and that she was only very lightly armed with two twin anti-aircraft guns and 4 or six smaller-calibre machine-guns.

This suggests that she was perhaps a small naval vessel from the First World War used for minesweeping duties and on which light armament had subsequently been installed.

The decks were in wood, a feature typical of small vessels and minesweepers.

The nationality of the vessel was something of a surprise: when the German crew came ashore after the sinking it was presumed that the ship herself had been German. You can imagine my surprise when a few years ago I found my way onto the bridge and cleared away the encrustation's on the engine-room telegraph and saw the French words "Avant" and "Arrière"... She was thus a French ship which had probably fallen into German hands following the occupation of France and put to work with a German crew, a common practice which also happened with the Italian ships after the 8th of September, 1943.

We turn now to the sinking of the *KT*. The ship was sailing off the Sestri Levante promontory, escorted by two anti-submarine motor boats on a cold February morning in 1944.

An allied submarine saw the ship through her periscope and launched two torpedoes, one of which missed its target and exploded on the coast close to the S. Anna tunnel.

The second struck the *KT* just astern of the funnel, sending her straight to the bottom. Nevertheless, it appears that there were no victims and that the frozen crew was eventually picked up by the two motor boats and

A

B

A - The KT at Sestri was sunk by a British submarine in April, 1944. She was a small French-built vessel requisitioned by the Germans. The ship, the prow of which can easily be seen in this photograph, is lying upright at a depth of 60 metres.

B - The KT was armed with two double-barrelled heavy anti-aircraft guns. This photo shows the fairly well preserved forward emplacement.

C - A diver is swimming close to the funnel which is still virtually intact in spite of the violent explosion which destroyed the stern section.

D - Parts of the ship, a capstan can be seen here, are frequently shrouded in clouds of red Anthias.

landed at Sestri. The *KT* sank
to the muddy sea-bed, and now
lies upright at a depth of less than
60 metres with the prow pointing
out to sea and the stern towards
dry land.

Diving to the wreck

The wreck of the Sestri *KT* is
one of the best and most
evocative not only of the
Mediterranean, but of the whole
world. There are, however, many
buts. It is a very deep dive, given
that you must always allow for a
descent as far as the sea-bed
lying at 60 metres.
The off-shore position of the
wreck also exposes it to currents
which on certain days may be
very strong. The whole of the
wreck is also covered in an
infinite tangles of lines, ropes
and nets which represent a
considerable risk, and the stern
is wrapped in an enormous and
diabolical trawl-net which is lifted
several metres high by its floats,
a deadly trapin the case of poor
visibility.
This is, therefore, a very
demanding dive and not advisable
for anybody other than expert
divers with plenty of experience,
including numerous dives to deep
wrecks. You should remember
that the difficulties involved in this
dive are a far cry from those in
clear tropical waters free of nets
and the dreadful mud which is
easily raised by the current or a
misplaced flipper. You can only
dive to the *KT* in excellent sea
and wind conditions and when
the water is warm, that is to say
in the summer months. You will
often find that you have to forego
diving even after having reached
the site. It is a dive with very little
margin for errors and has already
claimed a number of victims even
among experienced divers.
Your dive plan must therefore be
perfect. It is no good
approximating the position of the
wreck; once you have executed an
accurate echo sounding you must
drop a buoyed shot line over the
centre of the vessel and the cover
boat should follow your trail of air
bubbles, or anchor clear of the

E - The forward
section of the ship
with the
superstructure,
the bridge and
the cabins is in
excellent condition.
You still need to be
very careful,
however, due to the
great depth and the
strength of the
currents.

F - Along the
starboard flank, just
before the enormous
gash caused by the
torpedo which sent
the vessel to the
bottom, a double-
barrelled anti-
aircraft gun
identical to the one
at the prow, points
out into the
emptiness.

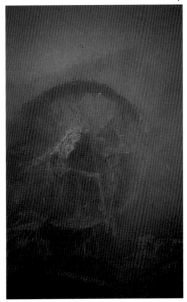

wreck so as not to damage it
(and so as not to risk losing the
anchor which in 7 times out of 10
would get caught up). You must
also plan for an adequate supply
of extra air at the decompression
stops, given that the depth of the
dive inevitably requires a
staggered ascent and a
considerable consumption of air
at the bottom. The descent is
thrilling, with a long fall into the
blue depths before you catch your
first glimpse of the wreck.
The highest part is a metal gantry
set on three feet on the
quarterdeck and reaching a height
of 35 metres from the surface.

If the sea conditions are good, the considerable distance from the shore ensures that the water is clear, at times even crystalline. In this case it is worth stopping at the top of the gantry allowing yourself time to acclimatise to the depth and to look over the entire wreck. What is immediately striking is the enormous quantities of fish, which surround the vessel, all moving as one with sudden bursts of activity which have the effect of making the whole wreck appear to be in motion. The funnel rises slightly further towards the stern, with the upper part of the metal cover missing and the internal pipes exposed. Below the gantry is the quarterdeck, with the

bridge accessible via a side door, but literally festooned with ropes of all kinds. The front openings are protected by a flap typical of naval vessels. The larger cabin below can be inspected from outside thanks to the numerous apertures and, with all due care, can be entered. The highly evocative engine-room telegraphs have been removed, together with other instruments, plates and on-board equipment, by certain divers who appear to interested in nothing else and are sadly lacking in respect and courtesy towards others. Fortunately, the depth of the wreck has dissuaded these individuals from taking away the vessel's armament, with the

A

B

C

D

A - A metal tripod rises from the quarterdeck to a point 35 metres form the surface. It probably carried the ship's radio aerial.

B - Close to the quarterdeck you will find a large steel unit with two shelves on which a number of semi-circular anti-aircraft cartridges are still stacked. This is an authentic and very well preserved rarity.

C - The omnipresent Anthias swimming around the feet of the antenna. The wreck of the KT is celebrated for the multitude of fish which have taken up residence.

D - Part of the wooden deck planking has rotted, and a number of rather insidious apertures have been created. You must pay attention where you put your hands and feet.

exception of one anti-aircraft machine-gun which has disappeared. The wreck is therefore still relatively intact, and offers a number of now rare sights. In the area of the quarterdeck you can see a two-storey container with semicircular anti-aircraft cartridges still lined up inside, and others scattered across the deck. The wreck's strong suit is represented by the twin anti-aircraft gun at the prow which has a calibre of perhaps 40.1 mm. It is mounted on the wooden deck within a circular shield. Apart from the integrity of the piece, what is particularly striking is the fantastic encrustation of actinia *(Corynactis viridis)* of a marvellous fuchsia shade. This organism can also be found on the deck and many other structures around the wreck in a broad range of colours from light green to red, from yellow to brown and itself makes the dive worthwhile. The prow, like the rest of the ship, is perfectly intact and it is worth swimming beyond the wreck so as to enjoy the sight of the narrow, sharp cutwater, and the two anchors drawn up to the hawser holes and a strange shield placed on the tip of the bow. If you want you take a look at the crew quarters located in the forecastle, but the wooden structure is now unstable which together with the large amount of sediment makes it unwise. You would be better advised to head towards the centre of the ship where there are other cabins, the engine-room and the boilers. All these areas should, however, be inspected without insisting on an internal exploration. Astern of the funnel, there is a clear step, typical of old naval vessels. Beyond this point, 9 times out of 10 there is nothing but a fog created by the current. There are actually the battered remains of the stern, with another twin anti-aircraft gun and circular shield, identical to the piece at the prow and overturned onto its right-hand side, and other machine-guns. Take great care however: a huge trawl net rises for some metres towards the surface, kept upright by its floats. It is better to turn back and ascend as far as the trestle which itself has, by the way, beautiful encrustations and on which some wonderful cerianthids are growing. From here you can take a final look at this fantastic wreck.

E - At the bottom of the gutted hold you can still see a number of bottles half-buried in the mud. You should be very careful when exploring this area as the stern is wrapped in a deadly trawl net and a web of lines and ropes.

F, G - Many plates are encrusted with splendid fuchsia corals (Corynactis viridis) and other multi-coloured organisms which are particularly suggestive in the semi-darkness of the wreck.

THE ARMED MERCHANT SHIP OF SESTRI
by Andrea Ghisotti

RATINGS

Location difficulty: average.
Visibility: from scarce to good.
Currents: from scarce to strong.
Diving difficulty: average.
Lines and nets: some.
Historical interest: average.
Photographic interest: high.
Biological interest: average.

DATA FILE

Type of wreck: armed merchant ship.
Nationality: German.
Date of construction: unknown.
Tonnage: 3,000 tonnes (approx.).
Date of sinking: November 1943.
Cause of sinking: torpedo.
Geographical co-ordinates:
    44°15'65" N, 9°23'21" E.
Localisation: 128° P.ta Manara,
    358° Sestri Levante tower.
Distance from shore: 850 metres.
Minimum depth: 27 metres.
Maximum depth: 36 metres.

THE ARMED MERCHANT SHIP OF SESTRI

In the November of 1943, a small German merchant ship was working the Italian coast and rounding the Sestri Levante Point. It was, armed as were most merchant ships in war time, so as to afford it at least minimal protection from enemy attacks. This vessel's principal armament probably consisted of a medium calibre gun located on the forecastle, together with another piece of artillery at the stern. There would also have been at least four anti-aircraft machine guns, the supports for which can still be seen

A

B

on the wreck. The ship was carrying a load of metals, mainly copper, a very precious material at the time, as well as a general cargo including ammunition of various types. This would explain the presence of large calibre shells lying on the sea bottom which are different to the smaller calibre ones found on the deck. The sinking was apparently the result of a surprise attack by a squadron of allied torpedo bombers. The explosion of the torpedo which struck the ship must have been devastating and the vessel sank immediately with her back broken. The two sections of the vessel now lie perpendicular to each other, separated by a mass of totally unrecognisable distorted metalwork. It is probable that there were victims

given the highly destructive effect of the torpedo which tore the vessel apart amidships. The wreck lies upright, with the stern section more or less parallel to the coast and the bow pointing out to sea. The sea bottom is muddy and level, but with a slight slope which accounts for the variation in depth from a little over 30 metres under the stern to 36 metres under the bow.

After the war many divers from a Leghorn salvage company worked on the wreck and further gutted the central section with explosive charges. One of the men tragically died during the operation.

The ship was also carrying mines and one of them was identified by the well known journalist Lino Pellegrini. He suffered an embolism

whilst shuttling back and forth between the wreck and the surface in order to photograph it. The mine was then exploded by the artificers and it too probably contributed to the destruction of the centre section of the ship.

Diving to the wreck

This is a dive of medium difficulty. The whole wreck can be explored whilst staying at a depth of around 28-30 metres, with an occasional descent to 36 metres to examine the wreckage scattered across the sea-bed. The ship is fairly long, however, and you will have to move quickly if you want to examine it from stem to stern. In my opinion it is better to dedicate two dives to the exploration of this wreck, looking at half the hull at a time.

This approach allows you time to take in all the small details.
It is better to look at the bow section, the best preserved and most evocative part, on the first dive. This section is slightly further out to sea and to the East of the stern. The descent should be made along shot line dropped over the centre of the wreck, and only on days with a calm sea and clear water given that it is some way from the coast and the current can be notably strong and reduce visibility. On fine summer days the wreck can be seen from the mid-way point of the descent. It is worth keeping a good watch as it is not rare to see sun-fish which happily cruise the decks of the ship.

On one particularly good day we saw no less than seven on one dive. Head straight for the bow. There are two ladders with hand-rails leading up to the forecastle which can be cleared with two flicks of your flippers. In the middle of the two is a companion-way leading to the crew-quarters below decks.
Air and light were provided by two skylights which are still in place. An impressive system of

chains and capstans leads to the tip of the bow. On the starboard side the deck is damaged, the result of a structural collapse due to corrosion, which allows the hull below to be seen. Moving into the open water above the bow you can admire the sleek, attractive design of the prow which represents one of the best photo opportunities provided by the wreck. If you spare a glance for the sea bottom you will see a series of large artillery shells, similar to others which can be found scattered around the vessel. Moving back to the deck you find the armoured shield of the main gun and a set of shells which have rusted together. Alongside these there also numerous semi-circular cartridges

C

D

E

from the four anti-aircraft guns which disappeared years ago. You can gain access to the holds via the gaping hole caused by the explosion amidships. The holds are, however, empty except for a few now unrecognisable wooden structures which crumble when they come into contact with air bubbles. The central area is a jumble of contorted plates and tubes, evocatively draped with numerous nets and lines. You are better off moving straight to the stern where you will find a large boiler, the engines and the quarterdeck, still intact and explorable, although a fairly tight fit and covered in a layer of mud. Lastly, a look at the rounded stern dug well into the bottom.

F

C - The good condition of the forward section of this still unidentified German wreck allows you to admire minor details such as this ladder leading to the forecastle.

D - A diver approaching one of the machine-gun supports mounted on the deck. You can also see numerous cartridges lying around.

E - The position of the wreck, lying upright on the sea-bed, makes the dive even more exciting. This photograph shows the handrail on the starboard side disappearing into the empty blue of the sea.

F - In order to explore the wreck in all its details you would be well advised to make two dives: one to the forward section and one to the stern. The photograph shows the forecastle and one of the skylights.

THE BARGE OF SESTRI
by Andrea Ghisotti

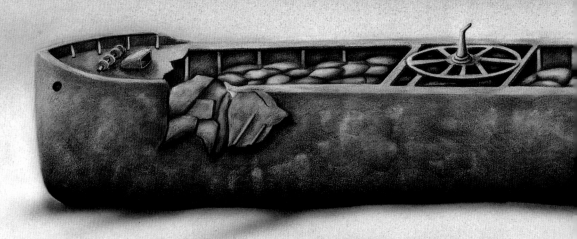

RATINGS

Location difficulty: average.
Visibility: from good to scarce.
Currents: scarce.
Diving difficulty: average.
Lines or nets: none.
Historical interest: average.
Photographic interest: average.
Biological interest: average.

DATA FILE

Type of wreck: barge.
Nationality: German.
Date of construction: unknown.
Tonnage: 300 tonnes (approx.).
Date of sinking: 1944.
Cause of sinking: aircraft
        bomb damage.
Geographical co-ordinates:
        44°15' 333" N, 9°23' 71" E.
Localisation: 33° Torre Sestri
Levante, 122° P.ta Manara.
Distance from shore: 850 metres.
Minimum depth: 26 metres.
Maximum depth: 31 metres.

THE BARGE OF SESTRI

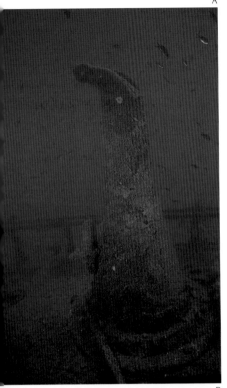

This story takes us back to the dark days of the Second World War, in late 1943 and early '44 with Italy occupied by German troops. Almost all the rail bridges along the Ligurian coast had been destroyed by bombing, and goods were frequently transported by sea along the coast, using whatever vessels available.

Numerous barges were constructed, and lighters similar to those used on the rivers with one or two open holds and one or two engines mounted at the rear were often adapted for use at sea. They were slow boats with maximum speeds of no more than four or five knots; Spartan and cheap, they were armed with a couple of machine guns so as to provide a token defence against enemy attacks.

The Italian coastal waters are full of the wrecks of these vessels which were sitting ducks for enemy aircraft, submarines and any ship with artillery.

The history of this barge is a little hazy and based on unconfirmed stories. It would appear to have been sunk in February, 1944, when it was heading South towards Deiva or the Cinque Terre with a load of cement which may have been destined to reinforce the defensive fortifications.

Whilst it was rounding the Sestri Promontory the air raid sirens sounded in the town. It was the usual "Pippo", the nickname given to the lone allied bombers which circled over the towns, especially at night, before releasing their bomb loads with devastating effects on the morale of the inhabitants.

This time the plane's target was the barge which was hit on the port side of the bow. A gash was opened up in the plating and it sank immediately.

The crew, four German sailors, had no chance; their bodies were washed up on the shore the following morning. They perhaps died of exposure.

Diving to the wreck

This is an easy dive given that the depth never exceeds the 31 metres at the stern of the barge, the deepest point. The wreck lies perpendicular to the coast with its bow turned to the land, almost as if it were making a desperate bid to escape from the attack. It is one of the most "expressive" wrecks I know of: you only have to examine carefully the details and the story and all the drama of the vessel's final moments coming flooding back. Given its small size (no longer than 35-40 metres), the best way to explore the wreck is to swim over it in open water so as to get a good idea of the layout of the structure, subsequently descending to examine the detail features. The bow is vertical and dumpy, ill-suited to coping with open seas. There are a number of cables on the foredeck, a capstan and a gangway leading to the anchor hold. On the port side you can see the gash which caused the barge to sink, with the plates distorted as if they were made of tin-foil. Moving towards the stern there are the two open holds, the second containing sacks of cement which are well and truly stuck together. Between the two holds is a full width metal platform which once carried the anti-aircraft gun. Unfortunately this has now disappeared but its moveable support remains. A number of cases of ammunition and a few loose rounds can be seen at the bottom of the hold and should be left alone. Having explored the second hold, and moving on towards the stern you come across

A - The barge of Sestri sank in February, 1944. In this photo you can see the support for one of the machine-guns which disappeared years ago.

B - A diver admiring the vivid colouring of a superb coral formation (Corynactis viridis) which almost completely covers the stern-rail.

the engine room, a fairly inaccessible area and consequently favoured by sargoes and lobsters. There then follows a structure which contained the galley. On the right there is a small three-ring stove with, at least up until 1993, a saucepan still in place over one of the rings, and another fallen to one side. It is a deeply touching sight: the crew were perhaps preparing their meal, something to warm them up on a cold February night, when they heard the drone of the aircraft. The bridge was exposed, with the engine room controls bolted directly to the bulkhead - they were simple boats do not forget. Lastly you reach the rear superstructure, the highest point of the wreck, reaching 26 metres at one point. Here the crew had their simple quarters and even though some of the plates have given way and part of the cabin has been opened up, a few years ago it was still possible to make another moving discovery: under the muddy sediment coating the interior a gramophone and a collection of 78's was found. Perhaps it was playing some German melody at the moment of the sinking. A second anti-aircraft position was installed above the crew's quarters which has again been pillaged. An accommodation ladder at the rear originally gave access to this position.

This is now the most attractive part of the wreck as much of the metal is covered with examples of one of the most beautiful marine organisms of the Mediterranean, a corallimorpharia known as the jewel anemone *(Corynactis viridis)* which lends a brilliant fuchsia pink tone to the barge, with the extremities of the tentacles tipped with white. Gliding along the ladder and over the hand-rail you find yourself swimming over the rounded stern which lies at 31 metres. The rudder has partially sunk into the mud, as the two propellers which are at least still in place. Between the hull and the sea bottom, behind the port propeller, a conger has made its home, and guards the wreck together with a colleague living in the engine room area.

C - *This photograph shows the sacks of cement which formed the barge's cargo. In all probability the cement was needed to reinforce the coastal defences at Deiva or the Cinque Terre.*

D - *It is always a thrill to find elements which evoke for a modern diver the drama involved in the sinking of a ship. In this photo you can see the barge's galley with a pot still in place on the stove.*

E - *This explosion of colour is fairly rare in the Mediterranean. These corals (Corynactis viridis)* are not very common, but are easily recognisable thanks to the characteristic form of their tentacles.*

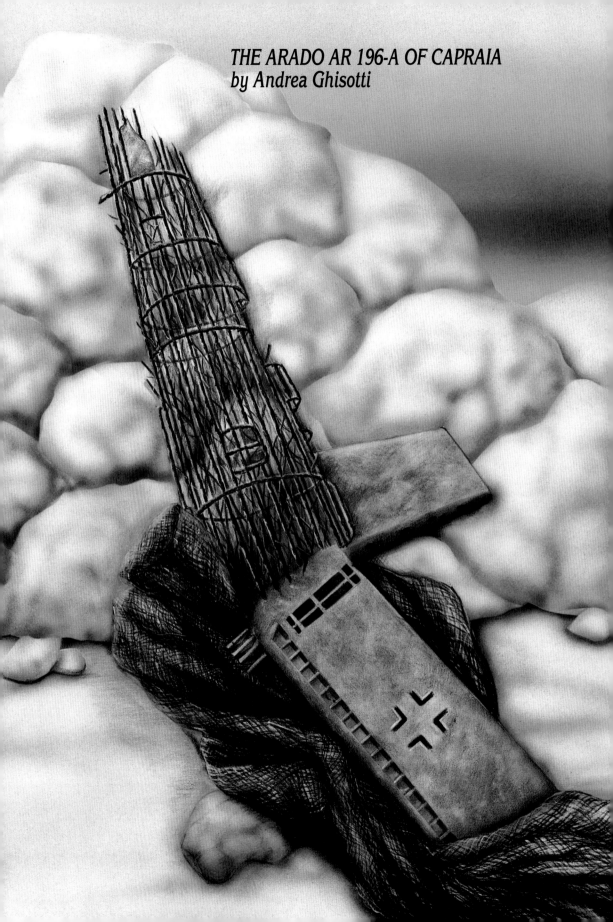

THE ARADO AR 196-A OF CAPRAIA
by Andrea Ghisotti

Teia Point **ARADO AR 196-A**
▼
Port
ISLAND OF • S. Giorgio
CAPRAIA Castle
(ITALY) Civitata
Point

Zenóbito
Point

FRANCE
ITALY
MEDITERRANEAN
SEA

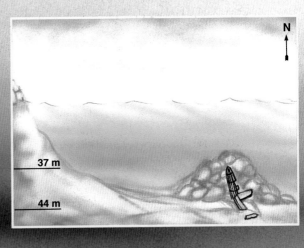

N

37 m

44 m

RATINGS

Location difficulty: average.
Visibility: excellent.
Currents: scarce.
Diving difficulty: average.
Lines or nets: some.
Historical interest: high.
Photographic interest: average.
Biological interest: average.

DATA FILE

Type of wreck: aircraft.
Nationality: German.
Date of construction: unknown.
Wingspan: 12.40 metres.
Length: 11 metres.
Weight at take off: 3,730 kilos.
Date of crash: 1943.
Cause of crash: unknown.
Geographical co-ordinates:
     43°02'74" N, 9°50'65" E.
Localisation: 181° Guglia P.ta Fica,
     223° Faro.
Distance from shore: 200 metres.
Minimum depth: 37 metres.
Maximum depth: 44 metres.

THE ARADO AR196-A

Directly in front of the village of Capraia, around 200 metres off-shore, there is a rocky outcrop extending out to sea, perpendicular to the coastline. There is an unusual wreck on the southern side of this rocky buttress, a German aircraft from the Second World War, the identification of which has been a long, fascinating search, partly caused by the trawl-net wrapped around the wreck. Only now have we reached a precise identification thanks to the assistance of Fabio Bourbon, a well informed aircraft enthusiast working for the publishers White Star. The plane is a small military aircraft, an *Arado Ar196-A* sea-plane of great historical value. Commissioned by the Kriegsmarine in 1936 to be carried on the principal German warships from which it could be catapulted, the *Ar196* went into production in 1939, with the *A-3* version dating from 1941. It is an example of the latter version which is lying in the waters of Capraia. This version had compound skin in fabric and aluminium which had for some time kept us guessing as to its identification as a spotter plane or a fighter. The wing of the *Arado* was covered in metal except for the control surfaces, as was the front section of the fuselage, whilst much of the rear fuselage was fabric-covered. There were two floats and the plane was armed with two MG FF 20 mm cannons housed in the wings and a MG17 7.9 mm machine gun in the left-hand front section of the fuselage and a second in the gunner's compartment (both may have been omitted in some versions). It also carried two 50-kg bombs below the wings. The date on which the plane was ditched is uncertain, it would appear to have been during 1943, in the period when the conflict on nearby Corsica was intensifying. The aircraft was equipped for coastal reconnaissance, and must have had problems which led to it being ditched in the waters of the Tuscan island. The point at which the plane crashed does not correspond with the point at which it is lying now.

The trawl-net must have dragged it from the surrounding sandy sea-bed and deposited it on the slope. The most probable scenario has the trawler crew struggling to land their unusually weighty catch and deciding to tow it to the shallower waters of the port. During the trip however, the net snagged on the rocks leaving the fishermen with no alternative but to cut the lines and abandon both the net and the plane. During the tow the wing was partially torn from the fuselage, and the very vulnerable floats which contained fuel were destroyed, but the main structures survived reasonably intact. As we analysed the details revealed in photos, our original hypothesis of a *Junker Ju. 87* dive bomber, better known as *Stuka*, was abandoned in favour of a much rarer aircraft produced in a total of just 493 examples, or 600 including the A-5 version produced at the end of 1943. Given the high historical value of the plane which was carried by famous ships such as the *Scharnhorst*, the *Gneisenau*, the *Graf Spee*, the *Lutzow*, the *Scheer* and the *Prinz Eugen*, we would strongly urge visitors not to remove anything at all from the site. This plea comes too late, however, to dissuade whoever it was that removed part of the instrumentation a few years ago.

A - A group of divers observing the metal structure of a German Arado *spotter plane partially shrouded in a net.*

B - This shot shows the ribs of the fuselage which were once covered in proofed fabric to render the aircraft lighter.

F

Diving to the wreck

This is quite a deep dive, at the limit for non-professional divers, as the nose of the aircraft is lying on a sandy bottom at 44 metres while the tail is at a depth of around 38-40 metres.
The duration of the exploration is restricted and you would be well advised to speak to the Capraia Diving Club instructors about the precise location of the wreck so as to avoid time-consuming searches. The water is almost always crystal-clear and after descending just a few metres you will see the higher part of the rocky outcrop. The aircraft is lying against the rock with its tail pointing upwards. It is worth moving away from the rock so as to get the best view of the wreck as a whole.
The fuselage of the aircraft has been reduced to a dense web of aluminium ribs and it takes some time to identify the main structures.
The aircraft is lying on its left-hand side with the cockpit openings turned towards the East. The rear cockpit, which maybe housed the gunner, contains a neat container with an opening hatch which was probably used to store ammunition or equipment. The forward cockpit is suggestive, with its instrument panel, the levers which controlled the air intakes, a number of knobs and the instruments.
Some of the dials are still there,

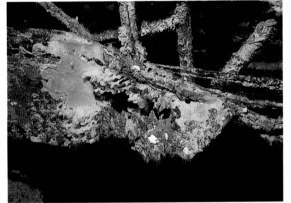

G

C - Little is known about why this aircraft crashed. Today it is lying at a depth of around 45 metres. This photograph shows what was probably the gunner's cockpit.

D - You can still see a metal chest with a hinged lid in the aircraft's cockpit.

E - The throttle levers and some of the instruments are still in place.

F - The whole of the German military plane is now encrusted with polychromatic sponges.

G - The German cross markings are still visible on one of the plane's wings.

although they have been torn out, others are missing all together.
The wing is massive, with one of the large machine guns visible from the breechblock side.
There are other interesting details: the catapult mounting, a hatch, another aperture, a kind of step up to the gunner's compartment and others.

The engine is also there, but as it is so hidden by the trawl net we would advise you not to bother looking for it.
On the other hand, you should take note of the many fish around the wreck, above all stonefish and the incredible tapestry of brilliant sponges covering the wreckage.

NASIM II
by Roberto Rinaldi

Secca Point

Cala Maestra

NASIM II
Punta
Pennello
Ischiaiola Bay

ISLAND OF GIANNUTRI
(ITALY)

Capel Rosso
Point

FRANCE

ITALY

MEDITERRANEAN
SEA

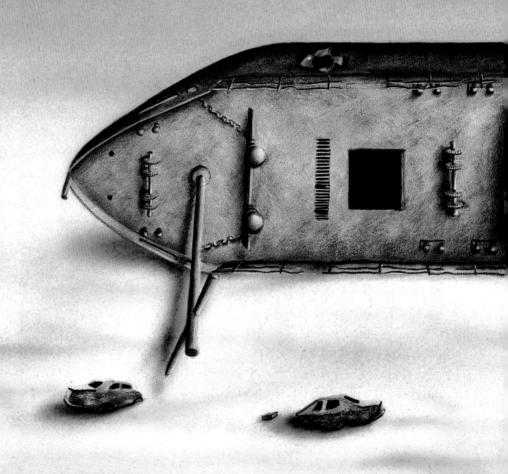

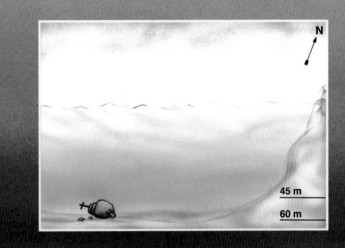

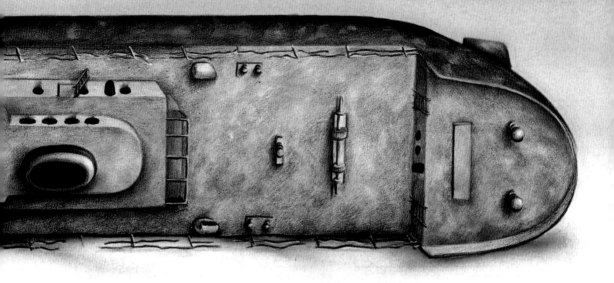

RATINGS

Location difficulty: average.
Visibility: usually very good.
Currents: none.
Diving difficulty: high.
Lines and nets: none.
Historical interest: low.
Photographic interest: average.
Biological interest: low.

DATA FILE

Type of wreck: ferry boat.
Nationality: Panamese.
Date of construction: 1959.
Tonnage: 700 tonnes.
Date of sinking: 2.12.1976.
Cause of sinking: collision
    against rocks.
Localisation: between Cala Maestra
    and Punta Pennello.
Distance from shore: about 100 metres.
Minimum depth: 45 metres.
Maximum depth: 60 metres.

THE NASIM II

It was the 11th of February, 1976, when the ferry *Nasim II* slipped her moorings at Leghorn and set sail for North Africa and the Egyptian port of Alexandria.
She was carrying around fifty cars and a number of trailers.
The eye-witness accounts suggest that the sea was calm that night,

A

B

D

A - From the forecastle you can look through the windows of the bridge. This photo was taken by pointing the lens upwards, taking advantage of the natural light.

B - A diver coming from the stern section of the wreck looks into a doorway.
He could only penetrate a few metres into the interior as the cabin is blind and completely empty.

C - This photograph shows the afterdeck of the Nasim II.
You can see the capstans which are still in good condition, as is the starboard ventilator.
A little further forwards, there are passageways to the crew quarters into which you can venture for a few metres.

D - Venturing beneath the port side of this ship is certainly exciting.
You pass between the sand and the plating until you reach the deck, where the currents have excavated a deep furrow in the sea-bed.

and yet at 4.30 in the morning the ship struck the rocks of Punta Scaletta and plunged to the bottom of the waters between Punta Pennello and Cala Maestra, very close to the shore.
At that time I was a novice diver, but I well remember the tales of the divers returning from the island of Giannutri with their hauls of car tyres, doors, seats and whatever else from the wreck and the vehicles in her cargo that was removable and saleable after

being rinsed clean. I also remember the tale of an old carpenter, presumably a witness to the ship going down.
He claimed that following the impact the crew tried to guide the vessel into the haven of Cala Maestra in a vain attempt to beach her and prevent her from sinking.
This would perhaps explain why the *Nasim II* is currently to be found lying on the sandy sea-bed with her prow pointing North

rather than South, the natural direction for a ship following her route. Perhaps the attempt to execute such a radical change of course combined with her considerable headway, resulted in the vessel making a complete inversion.
At the time she sank, the *Nasim II* was flying the Panamanian flag, but she had been built in the late Fifties in the shipyards of Brooke Marine Ltd. in England.
She had been afloat for a little

E

F

E - A diver is swimming below the great wreck of the Nasim II, close to a hatch leading to the galley as the colander lying on the sand suggests. It should be remembered that you would be very ill-advised to venture inside the ship.

F - Among piles of wood and the confused remains of furnishings, a delicate white spiral tube-worm appears to be trying to peer through the open windows of the bridge.

G - The propellers are usually the first goal for divers visiting this wreck; from here you swim up over the bulwark and, at lesser depths, along the deck.

H - This shot was taken inside the Nasim II: I very unwisely entered her in the early Eighties; now it would be even more dangerous due to the masses of cabling which over the years have detached themselves from the wall to form an insidious trap.

over fifteen years, therefore, when she struck the rocks off Giannutri and began to lose the cars loaded on her deck and to sink rapidly to the bottom.

Today she is lying on her port side with her bridge facing the open sea and her stern towards Cala Maestra, on a sandy sea-bed at a depth of around sixty metres. The cars she was carrying can be found scattered across the sea-bed at depths ranging from 30 to over 60 metres.

Diving to the wreck

The dive to the wreck of the *Nasim II* is very demanding is strictly reserved for experienced divers. Diving to the cars is a different matter, as it involves shallower waters and is also less difficult from technical and organisational points of view. My advice to those diving to the *Nasim II* for the first time is always to start off by visiting the cars as this will give you an idea of the conditions, and let you get to know the site before you begin your exploration of the wreck of the ship itself.

You should start from Cala Maestra, reaching the far side of the bay from the jetty by boat. On the very tip of the point you will see a small metal bollard on the rocks close to the water's edge.

You should moor here, over a sea-

G

H

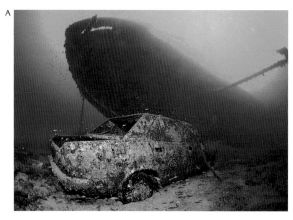

bed covered with sea grass.
After you have entered the water, follow the line of the sandy bottom of the bay and the bed of sea grass. As you keep the sand to your right, a brow will rise to your left. Follow the upper crest until you come across the first of the sunken cars balanced on the slope at a depth of around thirty metres. Below you the sea-bed is at a depth of 45 metres.

This is where what we jokingly call the "car-park" is to be found. The bottom is not perfectly flat, but slightly sloping out to sea and thus it is possible, as you move from one car to the next, to find your self in deeper waters than you had planned on.

The "car-park" can actually be visited by less expert divers as even though 45 metres is no mean depth, much of the dive

D - A cloud of minuscule Anthias animates the remains of a car.

E - The carcass of this car "parked" upside down, revives all the drama of the sinking of the Nasim II between the 11th and the 12th of February, 1976.

F, G - When diving to the Nasim II it is better to begin with the so-called "car-park". In this area the water is not excessively deep - up to 45 metres - you observe many of the 50 cars the ship was carrying.

A - This car, one of the many which fell to the sea-bed when the Nasim II sank, is lying at a depth of 60 metres, directly below the prow of the ship.

B - A diver is finning carefully so as not to disturb the sand and reduce visibility. Below him lies a car which sank close to the centre of the ship, just below the bridge.

C- The two cars lying on the sand at a depth of 55 metres between the ship and ridge, have become the home of numerous notably large scorpionfish.

can be completed at around thirty metres, and you can ascend from the bottom following the steep slope, soon finding yourself at the correct decompression depth. From there it is easy to return to the point where you left the boat, finning easily at a depth of three metres along the line of the rocky point.

Experienced divers can proceed from the "car-park" until they can see the enormous prow of the *Nasim II* through the clear water.

This first exploratory dive finishes here, at a depth of around 57 metres.
All that remains is to retrace your route, and with the site clear in your mind, begin planning your next dive. A boat equipped with an echo-sounder will make the use of land transits superfluous: all you need to do, in fact, is to begin from the shore and move out to sea for a couple of hundred metres and you will see the needle of the instrument jump from a depth of 60 to 48 metres. A useful reference point is formed by a group of natural fissures in the rock forming a triangle. Keeping this marker dead astern

F

E

G

and heading out to sea you will inevitably pass over the wreck.
In any case the transits indicated in the diagrams here will lead you to the prow of the wreck.
You should stop here, taking care to drop your anchor between the wreck and the coast, that is, of course, if you have no surface support capable of following your air bubbles.
If you do have a manned cover boat, take care: exhaust bubbles can easily be trapped below the *Nasim II*'s metalwork making it impossible for the surface crew to follow your movements.
Once anchored you can begin your dive. You should have to descend for no more than around 20 metres before making out the

side of the ship.
At this point you can leave the shot line and descend diagonally, aiming towards the stern of the ship, the deepest point and the most suitable from which to begin your exploration.
Your first photographs should be of the propellers and then you can fin along the deck, exploring the superstructure and looking in on the bridge.
There are very few apertures though which it is possible to enter the *Nasim II*, and even in these cases it is absolutely inadvisable to do so: they almost all lead into blind spaces, cluttered with forests of hanging electrical wiring and thousands of other potential dangers.

Having passed the bridge and moving on towards the prow, you find other cars lying on the sand. It is not worth descending to the sea-bed at 60 metres, it is better to use the time to pause at the tip of the ship's prow and examine the deep gash opened up in the keel by the impact with the rocks. At this point if you have planned your dive well, your anchor rope should be just above you enabling an easy, safe ascent.

ANNA BIANCA
by Roberto Rinaldi

Secca Point

Cala Maestra
ANNA BIANCA ▼
Ischiaiola Bay

ISLAND OF GIANNUTRI
(ITALY)

Capel Rosso Point

MEDITERRANEAN SEA

FRANCE

ITALY

RATINGS

Location difficulty: average.
Visibility: usually very good.
Currents: none.
Diving difficulty: average.
Lines and nets: none.
Historical interest: low.
Photographic interest: high.
Biological interest: average.

DATA FILE

Type of wreck: merchant ship.
Nationality: Greek.
Date of construction: unknown.
Tonnage: unknown.
Date of sinking: early 70's.
Cause of sinking: unknown.
Localisation: inside Ischiaiola Bay.
Distance from shore:
        about 150 metres.
Minimum depth: about 35 metres.
Maximum depth: about 52 metres.

THE ANNA BIANCA

We discovered the *Anna Bianca* years ago, back in the early Eighties. One evening after dinner, an old German sailing enthusiast first mentioned the existence of the wreck of a ship inside Ischiaiola Bay, to the South of Punta Pennello, and not far from the more well known wreck of the *Nasim II*, which had sunk four or five years earlier.

His description of the site and circumstances of the wreck appeared fairly far-fetched and vague, and smelt as false as his breath smelt of beer.

According to his story the ship exploded one calm winter's night without leaving any victims among her crew.

Following the sinking, as our old sea-dog recounted, a large quantity of white powder rose to the surface. Drugs. thought some who immediately started planning a salvage operation. "No, just pumice powder, part of the load transported by the freighter", replied the German. He claimed to have been on the spot at the time, and reckoned that the wreck would be lying at a depth of about 20 metres.

The next morning we went to talk to Costante Morbidelli, the owner of the Taverna del Granduca at Cala Maestra, a resident of the island for years and a more reliable source of information than the German.

He confirmed the facts, describing what happened one night in the early Seventies when he witnessed the death throws of the ship which had struck the rocks following a fairly violent storm.

The crew made it to safety and the freighter was left to the mercy of the waves for a few hours before sinking. The question was, where? Now that we were sure that the wreck existed, we stepped up our search. Costante was unable to provide us with a precise location, and so we began to comb Ischiaiola Bay in a series of

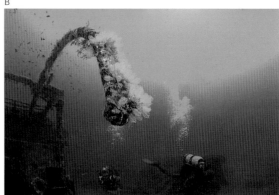

A - This shot allows us to admire the entire stern of the Anna Bianca. The clarity of the water off Giannutri and the compact dimensions of the cargo vessel make successful wide-angle photographs possible.

B - A dense group of tunicates covers the lifeboat derricks. Unfortunately these structures have collapsed, probably after having been struck by a boat's anchor.

C - A number of mooring ropes hang from a hatch at the stern. Just above, a spiral tube-worm has decided to anchor itself to the ship's plating.

breath-holding dives.
According to the German, the wreck should have been lying at a depth of about 25 metres, and would surely have been visible in the clear waters of Giannutri, if not from the surface then at least when diving a few metres without breathing gear.
We found the ship a few hours later, in front of a large cave.
I remember a great sense of disappointment: we were looking for a ship and what we had found appeared to be more the remains of a large motorboat.
It was, of course, a trick played by the limpid water.
What we thought when we dived just below the surface was a sea-bed at a depth of 25 metres, was in fact a full 40 metres down, and what we had found was a freighter and not a motorboat.

Diving to the wreck

A descent to 40 metres thus awaits you should you decide to visit the *Anna Bianca*. In spite of the depth, however, this dive is fairly easy if you anchor your cover boat directly over the wreck. It is, in fact, lying in a fairly sheltered bay in which we have never encountered strong currents, whilst the light sandy bottom contributes to providing the diver with a great sense of security which is further helped by the fairly compact dimensions of the wreck itself.

You leave from Cala Maestra and round Punta Pennello. You will immediately find the large cave and, a little further on, a villa on the cliff, with a large window overlooking the sea and steps carved into the rock leading down to the water.

The diagram of the transits taken off landmarks will help you to identify the correct point.

An echo-sounding may, nevertheless, be useful in confirming your position with respects to the ship.

You should lower the anchor between the wreck and the shore, and not the other way round, and you should not forget to let out plenty of rope to be sure that the anchor holds on the bottom.

You will spot the *Anna Bianca* after the first few metres, or at least you will spot the stern section of the vessel lying on its starboard side with the deck facing the shore. You will see the propeller shafts on the underside of the ship, but the propellers themselves have been removed. The sea-bed is at a depth of 40 metres, whilst the highest part of the wreck is at around 30. It is a small ship, therefore, and is easy to photograph in its entirety with a 15 mm lens, and is very photogenic thanks to articulated stern structures with their funnel and ventilators.

The lifeboat hoists collapsed a couple of years ago, a real pity as they were completely covered with transparent tunicates.

Approaching the stern you will come across a hawser poking out

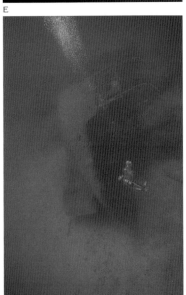

of a hatchway colonised by a big white spiral tube-worm. A little further on a pair of apertures give access to the engine room, but the space is too tight to be safe to enter. If you peer in with a torch you will find that it is inhabited by many conger and moray eels. Further on there is a mass of distorted plating, and then a metal structure lying on the sea-bed. It was probably the mess as the remains of the legs of the table fixed to the floor would suggest. You can enter a small bathroom via a small door. The toilet and wash basin are still

in place. Take a look at the toilet, it is inhabited by a moray eel and if it is not out hunting, you will find it in its unusual lair.

You can take good photographs in this area, taking advantage of the light filtering from above and the spiral tube-worms rising from the floor. Moving forwards, you find many distorted plates and the prow of the ship which is lying on the sand separate from the rest of the hull.

The depth here is over 50 metres and there is nothing else to see apart from ship's capstan.

We would thus strongly advise you not to insist on reaching this point, thus complicating what would be a relaxing dive, with no particular risk.

D - A little further towards the prow you find the funnel and the ventilators, as well as the entrance to the engine-room. Penetrating the interior of the wreck is difficult and very dangerous.

E - This photograph, taken from above the wreck, illustrates in detail the position and state of conservation of the freighter lying off Giannutri.

F - One of the numerous spiral tube-worms growing on the plates of the ship has in turn been colonised by a small bunch of squid eggs. In the background you can make out the stern profile of the Anna Bianca.

THE LST 349 MK. III OF PONZA
by Roberto Rinaldi

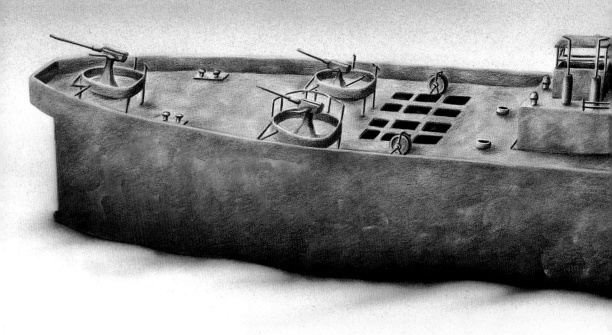

RATINGS

Location difficulty: minimum.
Visibility: usually very good.
Currents: none.
Diving difficulty: low.
Lines and nets: none.
Historical interest: average.
Photographic interest: average.
Biological interest: low.

DATA FILE

Type of wreck: landing ship tank.
Nationality: British.
Date of construction: 1942.
Tonnage: unknown.
Date of sinking: 2.23.1943.
Cause of sinking: bad weather.
Localisation: not far from
        Punta Papa.
Distance from shore:
        about 100 metres.
Minimum depth: 18 metres.
Maximum depth: 26 metres.

THE LST 349 MK. III

An *LST* is not the best of vessels in which to tackle a choppy sea. But it was just the job for the allied forces operating in the Mediterranean during the Second World War. In that period almost all the ports on the Italian peninsula and in the occupied territories were in the hands of the Axis forces. What was required for an invasion was a vessel with a very shallow draught capable of landing troops and vehicles on any beach. It was

B

C

D

for this reason that the British navy committed itself to the construction of great numbers of these vessels, 105 metres long, and 16 wide, with a draught ranging from 1.5 to 3 metres depending on the load. They were powered by two 5,500 hp engines providing a cruising speed of over 10 knots, and allowing over 200 crew and troops to be carried, as well as armoured vehicles and trucks. The landing ships were armed with two 40 mm cannons, and six 200 mm anti-aircraft machine guns to provide a measure of defence. The *Landing Ship Tank 349 Mk. III* which today lies off Punta Papa on the island of Ponza left Anzio in the night of the 22nd of February, 1943, bound for Naples carrying around 50 German prisoners, a number of vehicles and a certain quantity of munitions. The captain of the vessel knew full well that he could not tackle severe sea conditions, and with the wind rising and the waves getting ever higher, he decided to seek refuge below the cliffs of the island of Palmarola which offered reasonable shelter from the violent mistral. Unfortunately the engines were not up to the struggle with the elements and the ship was forced towards the island of Ponza. With the engines fading, the crew tried all they knew, dropping anchor near the Feola Bay. Even this last, desperate attempt to save the ship proved to be in vain as the violent waves tore away the moorings and began to batter

A -The stern section of the wreck, which sank around a hundred metres from the prow and is further inside the bay, appears to be threatening the diver to the left of the photograph.

B - The stern section, shown in this photograph, is less frequently visited, but still offers a number of elements of interest. This section is still upright and the main structures are fairly intact.

C - On the prow you can see the turrets still armed with machine-guns and cannons; one of these is visible behind the capstan in the foreground, lying on the deck.

D - The bow of the ship is the most heavily armed section as the cannons and machine-guns were designed to protect the disembarking men and vehicles.

the vessel against the rocks of Punta Papa. She eventually broke in two and plunged to the bottom, whilst the inhabitants of the island did all they could to rescue the survivors, throwing ropes and lifebelts into the sea.

In spite of their efforts there was a heavy loss of life. Over thirty bodies, prisoners and crew members, were found, together with that of the captain who committed suicide prior to the loss of his ship. It was a dramatic sinking which is in complete contrast to the tranquil atmosphere which now reigns around the wreck lying on a bed of white sand in clear waters.

Diving to the wreck

Locating the *LST* is very easy, all you need to do is make your way to Feola Bay and identify Punta Papa. You can moor your cover boat close to an emergent rock, not far from the rocks of the point itself. The wreck will be lying almost underneath you, and can easily been in the clear water.

A few fin strokes will take you to the bow section lying upright at a depth of around 26 metres. The bow door which lowered to allow men and vehicles to land, is no longer in place and thus a kind of tunnel has been created below the deck which has been embellished with colonies of beautiful yellow gorgonians, well fed by the currents which funnel into the interior. Having reached the wreck you will be faced with the temptation to go below the deck immediately: if you do your air bubbles will rise to the roof of the tunnel and begin to penetrate the many cracks in the plating and emerge on the deck, disturbing the sediment and ruining the possibility of good exterior photographs. It is far wiser to start with an exploration of the deck where the machine guns are still in place and turn smoothly on their supports. Here the depth is around 18 metres and so you can linger without any particular problems. The clarity of the water allows you to take successful photos of the entire section, as well as of

E - A diver is observing the unusual structures that were designed to protect the propeller and rudders.

F - The machine-guns and cannons mounted on the deck of the LST 349 Mk. III are a great attraction for wreck diving enthusiasts. The fact that they have resisted the corrosive effects of the water and can still be swivelled in all directions on their mounts makes them even more interesting.

the details like the guns and the doorway to a small cabin leading into the hold, a classic subject for all the photographers who have dived to this vessel. This is the most attractive section of the wreck, and many divers do not even realise that the stern section still exists, and is to be found lying around 100 metres away towards the bay. It is possible to locate it even whilst underwater by following the trail of wreckage scattered across the sea-bed, and by using your intuition. It is, however, preferable to make a second dive to the stern, even though I have to say that it is less interesting than the bow. Here you are within the bay and the maximum depth is no more than 20 metres. The stern section is also lying upright, even though much of it is buried in the sand. Some of the deck structures are still in place, but the cabins are now almost completely filled with sediment and it would be very unwise to try to enter them. It is a much better idea to fin over the wreck, an ideal subject for successful wide-angle photographs.

G - The deck structures at the stern suffered considerable damage when the boat sank as well as the effects of corrosion.

SANTA LUCIA
by Roberto Rinaldi

SANTA LUCIA ▼

VENTOTENE ●

ISLAND OF VENTOTENE
(ITALY)

Arco Point

RATINGS

Location difficulty: high.
Visibility: usually very good.
Currents: sometimes.
Diving difficulty: from average to high.
Lines and nets: some.
Historical interest: average.
Photographic interest: average.
Biological interest: average.

DATA FILE

Type of wreck: ferry boat.
Nationality: Italian.
Date of construction: unknown.
Tonnage: unknown.
Date of sinking: 7.10.1943.
Cause of sinking: torpedo
            bombers attak.
Localisation: close to rocks
            of Sconciglie.
Distance from shore: about 2 miles.
Minimum depth: about 39 metres.
Maximum depth: about 46 metres.

N

39 m

46 m

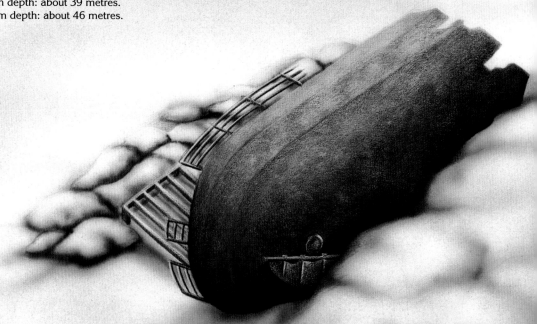

THE SANTA LUCIA

The wreck of the *Santa Lucia* can rightly be considered a war wreck, even though she was not strictly a military ship. The *Santa Lucia* was a humble ferry, one the "mail boats", as they was called by the inhabitants of the small islands they connected with the mainland. Back on the 10th of July, 1943, the "mail boat" left Ponza in the direction of little island of Ventotene where it was due to take on further passengers. There were already over a hundred people on board, including a newlywed couple.

The ship had almost reached Ventotene where another hundred people were waiting, when a group of seven allied aircraft appeared in the sky.

Captain Simeone thought that they were fighters and ordered the crew and passengers to take cover below decks whilst the first bursts of machine-gun fire were already whipping across the ship. Unfortunately the planes were not fighters, but rather torpedo bombers: it was the last plane that launched the torpedo which struck the *Santa Lucia* amidships. She broke in two and sank like a stone in front of the stunned eyes of those waiting on the quay at Ventotene whose fortune it was not to have already boarded the ship. None of those who were below decks had any chance of escaping from the disaster. Captain Simeone's last, desperate efforts to save the ship by running her aground on the shallows surrounding Ventotene were in vain. "I did my best to put her onto the rocks" were his last words to a fisherman who was attempting to save him. Today the prow of the *Santa Lucia* is still turned towards the island, just as Simeone had set her before the sinking.

Diving to the wreck

It is by no means easier to pin her down without precise co-ordinates given that she is lying a couple of

miles off the coast of Ventotene, on a flat sea-bed at a depth of over 40 metres. An aid to finding the exact position is that of aligning Punta Eolo with the centre of the Bourbon jail on the island of Santo Stefano and moving along that line until the town hall appears behind the point.

A precise echo sounding will be useful once you have reached the area given that the shape of the wreck stands out well against the flat sea-bed.

Once you have found the site, drop the anchor taking care to let out enough rope to allow it to take hold on the sandy bottom. Descending along the rope through the clear water you will immediately notice alternate light and dark patches on the bottom; the area is in fact covered with white sand, with scattered rocks and clusters of sea grass around the dark mass of the wreck.

The ship is broken in two, with the bow section lying upside down and pointing towards Ventotene. There follows a mass of deformed, distorted metal which was probably the point hit by the torpedo and ruptured by the explosion. A little further on, at almost 90° to the bow, you will find the stern section, lying on its port side and still reasonably intact.

The spectacle of the clouds of fish around the wreck will enchant you

A - The small stern of the ferry Santa Lucia, *lying on her port side on a sandy sea-bed. There is still much to be seen on her deck, including a number of capstans and the handrails.*

B - A diver is observing the upturned prow which is located some distance from the centre section of the vessel.

C - At the prow you can clearly see the two anchors, still in place in the hawse-holes. The vessel was, in fact, underway when it was attacked by the British torpedo bombers. The bow section must have sunk very quickly, given that the anchors had no time to shift from their housings.

D

E

F

D - The central section of the Santa Lucia has been reduced to a mass of scrap metal forming a link between the bow and stern sections. In spite of the tremendous explosions and the sinking of the vessel, the glass in this porthole has miraculously survived intact.

E - Finning over the deck you come across this mooring bollard now completely encrusted.

F - A diver swimming under the prow of the Santa Lucia; again you can see the great anchor chain hanging from the port hawse-hole.

from the first few metres of the dive. There are great numbers of red and black damselfish, dense schools of sardines, clouds of saddled sea breams, and occasionally groups of tuna.

At one time a gigantic grouper was the undisputed queen of the ship, but it has not been spotted by any one for some time.

If you are lucky you might also come across the large and pacific Saint Peter fish and two sun-fish spotted throughout last summer. Having reached the bottom you should move directly towards the stern which, lying at a depth of

46 metres, is the deepest area that you will reach on this dive. You will find the poop deck cluttered with capstans and superstructures of various kinds. The rail is still in good condition and is good subject matter, but t he propeller is trapped between the hull and a rock is thus difficult to photograph.

Here you will often see a large conger and a family of corvinas. Take care when exploring the after section as it is here that the lines and remains of nets lost by fishermen are concentrated.

Moving on you will find the plating described earlier.

You should be careful when looking between the metal and the sea-bed as many fish take refuge in these niches.

You will also find an intact porthole still set in the metal plates which makes another good photo opportunity.

You then reach the up-turned bow section of the ship where you can photograph the large anchors still

set in place in their hawses. You could also photograph the entire forward section with one of your diving companions included in the shot to give an idea of scale. You can then look at what little there is to be seen of the deck between the wreck and the sea-bed. You should use a powerful torch and try to move as quietly as possible as a large family of corvinas lives among the large capstans and the anchor chains which are now resting on the sandy bottom.

This brings the dive to an end, and all that remains is to ascend along the anchor rope to the cover boat glancing back at the wreck visible through the crystalline water.

ANGELIKA
by Andrea Ghisotti

Punta
Marmorata

Testa
Cape

SANTA TERESA
DI GALLURA

ANGELIKA

S A R D I N I A
(ITALY)

Pozzo
Port

FRANCE

ITALY

MEDITERRANEAN
SEA

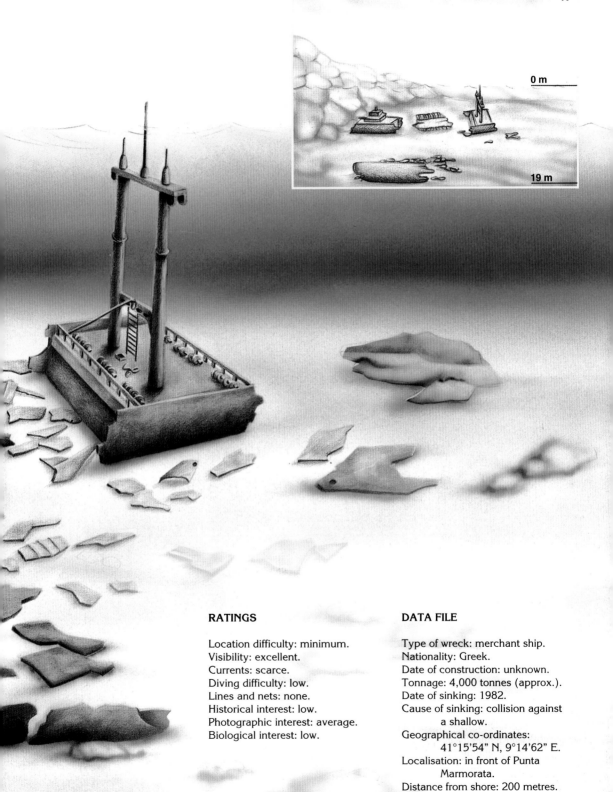

N

0 m

19 m

RATINGS

Location difficulty: minimum.
Visibility: excellent.
Currents: scarce.
Diving difficulty: low.
Lines and nets: none.
Historical interest: low.
Photographic interest: average.
Biological interest: low.

DATA FILE

Type of wreck: merchant ship.
Nationality: Greek.
Date of construction: unknown.
Tonnage: 4,000 tonnes (approx.).
Date of sinking: 1982.
Cause of sinking: collision against
     a shallow.
Geographical co-ordinates:
     41°15'54" N, 9°14'62" E.
Localisation: in front of Punta
     Marmorata.
Distance from shore: 200 metres.
Minimum depth: surface level.
Maximum depth: 19 metres.

THE ANGELIKA

A

Mariners tend to look on the Strait of Bonifacio, considered to be one of the most tumultuous areas of the Mediterranean, with reverential respect and a touch of apprehension.

Two seas meet in this Strait, the Tyrrhenian and the Sea of Corsica and Sardinia, both of which are very deep.

The Strait, on the other hand, has a depth no greater than 80 metres in the narrowest section.

You can well imagine the intensity of the currents, veritable rivers,

A - In this photograph you can clearly see the structure needed to support the block and tackle used for the loading of the cargo. The highest part emerges above the surface making the wreck easy to locate.

B

B - The exploration of the Angelika *is easy as there are no strong currents, allowing you to examine the interior of the ship.*

C - During the dive you reach the three-bladed propeller close to the sandy bottom. As you can see in this shot, the blades are distorted; it was undoubtedly turning at the moment of impact and struck the rocks.

C

D - The rays of sunlight filtering down from the surface highlight the profile of the encrusted handrail at the stern, and the bollards around which the mooring lines ran.

D

to which must be added the violence of the conflicting mistral and libeccio winds which are only occasionally dominated by the scirocco.

Given that both the Corsican and Italian waters are punctuated by many shallows and outcropping rocks the heavy toll paid over the centuries by shipping in the area is understandable. Wrecks from all eras stud the sea bottom and at certain points you can even find modern wrecks overlying fragments of Roman amphorae, the rusty hulks of freighters and steamers which went down in successive periods.

There have been terribly dramatic incidents such as the painful and unforgettable sinking of the great French frigate *Sémillante* which struck the rocks of the Lavezzi islands in 1855 while she was on her way to the Crimea with almost 800 troops on board.

None of the crew or soldiers survived. Other stories have a happier ending with entire crews being saved and only the insurance companies being left to shed a tear over the loss of another ship.

This was the case with the *Angelika*, one of the many Greek freighters navigating the seas and oceans, which had the misfortune to fall foul of the violence of these waters.

The incident took place in 1982 when the ship was in the area with a cargo which officially comprised sugar and other foodstuffs, but which typical shipwreck legend has transformed into less innocuous material.

Dangerous substances in this case, drums of pollutant waste products which are said to have prevented the ship from docking at Santa Teresa di Gallura.

The ship was battered by the waves off Punta Marmorata, a headland surrounded by a series of rocks and islands and a series of shallows of various depths, an anathema for coastal shipping. It is not known whether a mechanical problem or a navigation error led to the *Angelika* running violently aground in one of these shallows and being left high and dry and at the mercy of the elements. The crew, numbering around 20 in total, succeeded in reaching safety and were provided with accommodation in the few hotels open out of season at Santa Teresa. In the meantime the sea completed its destructive work with incredible efficiency, transforming the ship into a jumble of metal plates dispersed over a vast area of the sea bottom. The wreck is easily located as a mast still sticks out of the water to a height of around four metres.

Diving to the wreck

Diving to the *Angelika* is not particularly demanding thanks to the vicinity of the coast and the limited depth ranging from surface level to a maximum of around 20 metres.
You may come up against currents on certain days, however, and this makes things more difficult.
The *Angelika* is, nevertheless, one of the most frequently visited wrecks as the Cala Marmorata, the bay opening to the South of the island of the same name, houses a Club Mediterranée complex which brings boatloads of divers to the site each day.
The dive can begin just off the shore where the first metal plates are to be found, or directly from the emergent mast from which the expanse of wreckage can be seen.
The mast is fixed to the centre of a gantry used for loading and unloading the cargo, a kind of inverted U-shaped structure from which numerous block and tackle sets hung, operated by a series of capstans which can still be seen at the foot of the structure.
The overall view is evocative, and undoubtedly represents one of the wreck's most interesting photo opportunities.
Swimming southwards over demolished plates you reach the rear quarterdeck which is worthy of careful examination, being separated from the rest of the ship and intact.

E

F

G

E - The exploration of the severely damaged, but still evocative wreck continues with the large capstans located at the base of the loading derricks.

F, G - These photosgraphs show details and a panoramic view of the interior of the quarterdeck which you should visit, even though it is practically empty.

Many of the doors and windows lead into the interior of the bridge and the other cabins which can easily be explored, and in which excellent photographs can be taken thanks to the attractive play of light created.
The exploration of the wreck continues by proceeding further off-shore where the remains of the ship are partially intact.
The engine can be seen lying on the sea bottom, whilst a large tank similar to a boiler is still housed in the hull.
The stern section is lying on its left-hand side, with the hand-rail still intact, its large bollards and the three-bladed propeller now touching the bottom.
The propeller is large.
The blades are distorted which would suggest that it was still turning at the moment of impact, and that it might have been the first part of the ship to strike the bottom before seizing and leaving the ship to its fate.
The rest of the hull has been demolished and is all but unrecognisable.
However, it still represents testimony to the power of the sea and its destructive strength.

THE VOUGHT F4U CORSAIR OF CAPO COMINO
by Egidio Trainito

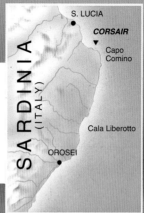

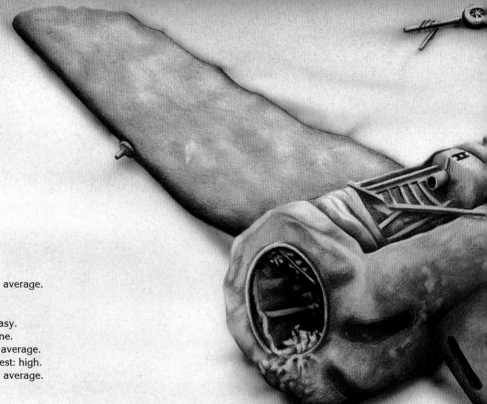

RATINGS

Location difficulty: average.
Visibility: good.
Currents: scarce.
Diving difficulty: easy.
Lines and nets: none.
Historical interest: average.
Photographic interest: high.
Biological interest: average.

DATA FILE

Type of wreck: air fighter.
Nationality: French.
Date of construction: unknown.
Wingspan: 12.5 metres.
Length: 10.16 metres.
Weight at take off: 5,950 kilos.
Date of crash: perhaps 1956.
Cause of crash: technical problems.
Localisation: in the centre of the bay
        North of Capo Comino.
Distance from the shore:
        about 300 metres.
Minimum depth: 4.5 metres.
Maximum depth: 6 metres.

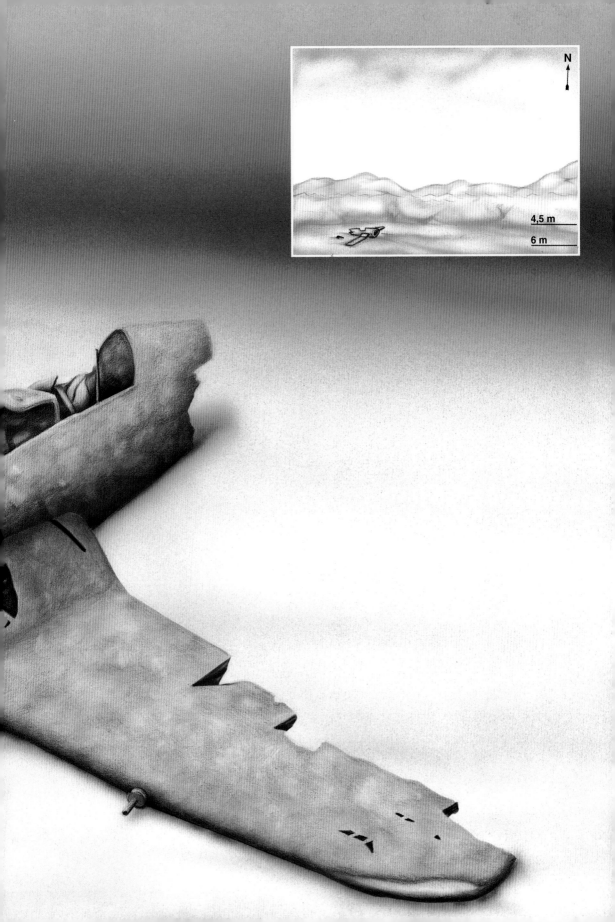

4,5 m

6 m

N

THE VOUGHT F4U CORSAIR

The history of the *Corsair* at Capo Comino is uncertain and in some respects legendary. The aircraft appears to have crashed into the sea due to mechanical problems in the mid-Fifties. It took off from Toulon airfield, had perhaps refuelled at Ajaccio and was heading for Saigon in Indo-China, making an unknown number of further refuelling stops along the way. The plane was ditched off the Eastern coast of Sardinia and sank to the deep sea bottom. It would still be there had it not been caught in a trawl net and dragged to the shallows in front of the beach at Salina Manna. At that point the aircraft was virtually intact, but it was not long before the usual predators began the systematic removal of souvenirs. These were souvenirs on a grand scale given that one of the first components to be taken away was the large radial engine and the propeller.

The story goes that among the things found and removed, apart from the joystick, the instrumentation, was a human skull. Not that of the pilot but rather one that the pilot took along as a lucky charm.

The truth? Legend? It takes just a few years for it to become virtually impossible to unravel the various stories recounted by "those in the know". The *Vought F4U Corsair* was a low-wing monoplane with a characteristic gull-wing frontal aspect.

Six principal versions were constructed with 18-cylinder twin radial engines and one with a 28-cylinder engine arranged in four radial blocks.

The prototype made its maiden flight in 1940, and the model was subsequently built in the USA from 1942 to 1953, with over 12,000 examples coming off the production lines. It was 10.16 metres long, had a wingspan of 12.50 metres, an operating ceiling of 11,000 metres and a range of

around 1600 metres. Although it was normally armed with 6 Browning 12.7 mm machine-guns, the version lying off Capo Comino was equipped with four 20 mm cannons. This model could also carry 1,814 kg of bombs and rockets below the wings, and it featured cockpit and fuel tank armour.

The *Corsair* was the best naval fighter of the Second World War, and perhaps the finest USA fighter, rivalled only by the *Mustang*. It was also the first American aircraft to overcome the 400 mph barrier.

It was capable of operating from both land and aircraft carriers and carried just the pilot, crammed

A - The Vought F4U was undoubtedly the best carrier-borne fighter of the Second World War; 12,681 examples of the Corsair were produced, and the plane remained in service until 1965. During the war in the Pacific theatre, 2,140 enemy aircraft were downed for the loss of just 189 Corsairs. In this archive photograph you can clearly see that the Corsair's wings could be folded so that it could be parked in the carrier's hanger.

B - The tail of the wrecked plane is missing. It has not been possible to establish whether it broke off when the plane hit the water, or whether it was perhaps caught up in a trawl-net which dragged the plane to its present position.

C - The Corsair at Cape Comino is lying on a sandy sea-bed that is continually shifting. In this photo the wings are exposed and the whole aircraft is visible.

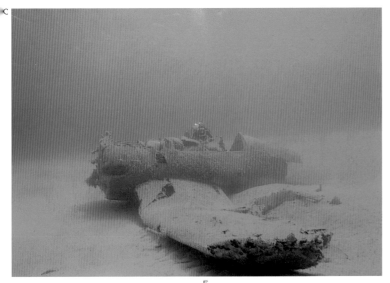

into the small cockpit: perhaps the plane's only defect was its restricted field of vision. With good reason, the Japanese nick-named the *Corsair* "Whispering Death". During the 64,000 missions flown in the Pacific theatre, the USA fighters downed 2,140 enemy aircraft for a loss of only 189 units. The Capo Comino wreck is one of the *94 F4U-7*'s bought by the French airforce and used in Indo-China and during the Suez crisis in 1956, and subsequently kept in service until 1964.

Diving to the wreck

The aircraft is lying the right way up on a sea-bed of white sand at a depth of 6 metres. It is not easy to locate, but given the shallowness of the water once you have reached the area all you need to do is fin up and down and you will spot it. A line and float is often attached to the wreck and in this case you will have no problems as there are no other buoys in the area. Reaching the wreck from the front, it appears ready to fly up, especially when you are fortunate enough to visit it after a high tide has swept all the sand off the wings. It is a pity that the engine and propeller are missing. The white sand reflects the light with great intensity and allows the smallest details of the plane to be examined.

The *Corsair* has a pair of custodians: two trigger fish, located in the cockpit, which defend their territory. Here there is still a tangle of electrical wiring, levers and other instruments. A length of net is still caught up around the seat. The four 20 mm cannons are visible in the wings,

and on the left-hand wing there is a plate carrying technical data. The tail is damaged and lacks the rudder and tailplane. Through the damaged section you can see structural elements. There are still traces of the roundel of the French airforce on the fuselage.

D - A length of net is entangled in the cockpit, but you can still see the tubes and cables of the controls. The fuel tank is still in place in front of the cockpit.

E - The cockpit of the *Corsair* was perhaps the plane's only weak spot, as the pilot had only a very restricted field of vision.

F - The rear centre section of the left-hand wing has been gashed and tubes and cabling and a cannon have been exposed. The *Corsair* was armed with 6 machine-guns or, as seems to be the case with this example, 4 20-mm cannons.

THE KT OF OROSEI
by Egidio Trainito

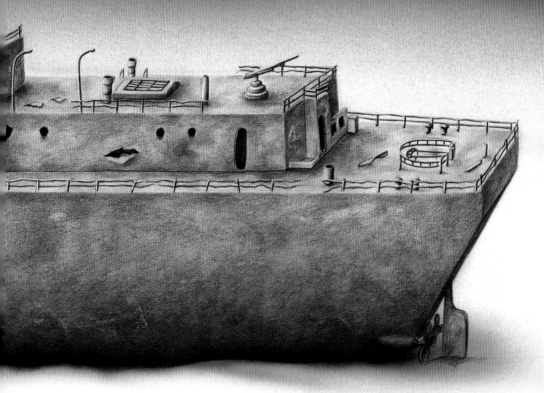

RATINGS

Location difficulty: high.
Visibility: good.
Currents: often strong.
Diving difficulty: high.
Lines and nets: none.
Historical interest: high.
Photographic interest: high.
Biological interest: average.

DATA FILE

Type of wreck: military cargo.
Nationality: German.
Date of construction: unknown.
Tonnage: unknown.
Date of sinking: 1943.
Cause of sinking: torpedo.
Localisation: off the coast of Osalla-
        Marina, Orosei, Sardinia.
Distance from the shore:
        about 2 miles.
Minimum depth: 20 metres.
Maximum depth: 34 metres.

A

A - This archive photograph shows the British submarine Safari, particularly active along the East coast of Sardinia in 1943. This submarine was responsible for the sinking of the KT at Orosei and at least three other vessels.

B - The stanchion which ran along the flanks of the KT is now completely covered by various flourishing bentonic organisms.

C - Along the deck on the port side you can still see the lifeboat derricks. In the background you can make out the superstructure at the stern.

The German convoys and cargo ships supplying the troops stationed in North Africa sailed along the Eastern coast of Sardinia. It was no easy passage as that area of sea was patrolled by the British submarines which, especially towards the end of the conflict, could count on a land-based information network which allowed them to predict the movements of the convoys and thus to intercept them.

The most famous of these submarines was the *Safari*, the vessel responsible for at least four of the wrecks on the Sardinian East coast. The Orosei *KT* was intercepted by the *Safari* in 1943; she tried to run the blockade, opening fire with her cannons and machine-guns.

They were of course rather ineffectual compared with the torpedoes with which the submarine replied.

The enormous gash in the bow of the wreck bears testimony to the devastation caused by the torpedo. An explosion ripped open the hull and set the ship ablaze. She sank rapidly; many of the crew lost their lives and the entire mixed cargo went to the bottom. The large bow hold of the *KT* still contains a number of drums which once held fuel.

The older inhabitants of Orosei call the wreck "the petrol tanker" as almost all of the drums not damaged by the explosion were washed up on the shore, or salvaged and hidden below the sands of the beach at Osalla.

In the immediate post-war years, those living in the Orosei area used that fuel to run tractors, boats and all kinds of engines. The "petrol tanker" was also carrying trucks, motorcycles, armoured cars, cranes and sanitary supplies, shoes, all destined for the troops at the front. The "petrol tanker" was armed with machine-guns and a cannon on the poop deck. The German-built ship was a *KT*, that is a landing craft with a flat bottom, around 70 metres long and 11 metres wide.

Diving to the wreck

The wreck of the *KT* is lying around 2 miles off the Orosei Marina and it is not easy to locate with transits taken off landmarks. Neither are the echo-soundings easy to interpret for the inexperienced.

There are frequently strong currents in this area, and so it is very easy to lose the trace just as soon as you have found it.

Once you have located the wreck and begun your dive you realise that your efforts were worthwhile, as the *KT* proves to be an ideal wreck. It is lying upright on a sandy bottom at 35 metres, with the tallest structures at around 20 metres.

The upper decks are still partially erect. A large metal plate which covered a structure on the top deck has slipped to the sea-bed, taking with it the machine-gun supports.

B

C

Towards the stern, the cannon is pointing towards the surface and close by you can see the helm and a hefty anchor.
The rounded stern is very evocative and the two propellers are still in place.
You can reach the engine compartment via the poop deck, but you must be very careful as there is a tangle of tubes and cables. Pressure gauges and other instruments are still in place. Many objects are scattered around the wreckage, and many more have already been removed by the usual

scavengers: helmets, boots, boot soles, a knife made at Solingen, various pots and pans, gas masks... There is still much to be discovered and as you are examining the structures remaining on the decks, you will find that a school of amber jacks will begin to swim around you. If you remain motionless their dance will go on for some time. Along the starboard flank, two mobile cranes are laying on the sea-bed, still fitted with their tyres, together with an armoured car with thick glass.
The quantity of objects scattered across the sea-bed and in the various parts of the wreck, and the dimensions of the ship mean that you need to make many dives if you want to examine everything. The cabin area is intact, but stripped bare, and you can move though it.

Above the cabins is the bridge looking out towards the bow.
It can be entered either via the hatchway on the deck, or through the gash torn by the torpedo at sea-bed level.
As soon as you enter the hold you will meet a school of corbs which will immediately seek refuge in the inaccessible areas. There still many oil drums on the floor: they are the few that remain of the hundreds that once filled the hold.
Swimming out of the hold via the hatchway on the deck you find yourself facing the bridge: seen from this angle it seems intact and ready to steam off from one moment to the next.
Returning towards the stern along the port side deck, you can see the lifeboat hoists which still remain standing.

D - There are two funnels at the stern above the engine-room, with two hatches alongside covered with gratings. In the foreground of this photograph you can see an anti-aircraft gun which has fallen from its mounting.

E - The cabin structures are still standing, but have been reduced to a framework of girders and distorted, encrusted panels. Now completely empty, the interior can be visited fairly easily.

F - At the gashed bottom of the hold there are still numerous drums of the fuel which formed part of the KT's cargo and which during the war earned the vessel the nick-name "the petrol-tanker of Orosei".

ROMAGNA
by Egidio Trainito

SARDINIA
(ITALY)

Cagliari Pond

CAGLIARI

CAPITANA

Gulf of Quartu

S. Elia Cape

▼ **ROMAGNA**

Gulf of Cagliari

FRANCE

ITALY

MEDITERRANEAN
SEA

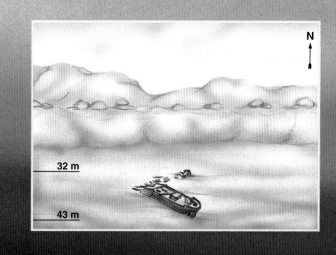

RATINGS

Location difficulty: average.
Visibility: good.
Current: occasionally strong.
Diving difficulty: high.
Lines and nets: some.
Historical interest: high.
Photographic interest: average.
Biological interest: average.

DATA FILE

Type of wreck: tanker.
Nationality: Italian.
Date of construction: 1899.
Tonnage: 1,416 tonnes.
Date of sinking: 8.2.1943.
Cause of sinking: mine.
Localisation: about 1.5 miles out
        of the port of Capitana.
Distance from the shore:
        about 3 miles.
Minimum depth: 32 metres.
Maximum depth: 43 metres.

THE ROMAGNA

In 1943, the year of the armistice, Sardinia witnessed a dramatic increase in air and naval conflicts which also affected the populations of many of the island's towns. The Gulf of Cagliari hosts the wrecks of entire convoys, freighters, tugs, smaller vessels and aircraft, all displaying the damage caused by mines and torpedoes. What follows is the story of one of these vessels, the *Romagna*, an old 1,416-tonne tanker built in 1899 and requisitioned by the Italian navy at Cagliari on the 4th of October, 1941. On the 2nd of August, 1943, the tanker was carrying a load of fuel destined for Cagliari: it was of strategic importance for the military vehicles, and especially the aircraft, involved in the defence of the island.
The *Romagna* was escorted by six small anti-submarine vessels, with air cover being provided by two pairs of Macchi 202's and 205's from the 51st fighter squadron. The coastal anti-aircraft batteries in the Gulf of Cagliari at Prunas and Faldi were at a state of alert from 7.53 in the case of enemy aircraft attacks and were monitoring the progress of the ship. At 8.07, when she was just a few miles out of the port of Cagliari, the *Romagna's* bows struck a mine that had recently been laid as part of a defensive barrier and had probably not yet been marked on her charts. From the beginning of the conflict, over 5,000 mines were laid in the Gulf of Cagliari and along the Sardinian coasts. The explosion of the mine blew the prow of the ship clean off, ignited the fuel and stopped the ship dead. She then drifted out of control. Whilst the aircraft returned to base after having executed many passes in search of a possible enemy submarine, the escort ships approached the *Romagna* in the hope of picking up survivors. They were forced to turn away however, because at 8.39 they were attacked by *American Curtiss P40* and *P38 Lightning* fighters.
After the air-raid warning had been

A

B

C

lifted, the Faldi coastal battery spotted a boat close to the wreck with two survivors signalling for help. They were rescued just before another air attack at 10.20.
In the meantime the *Romagna*, devastated by the fire and the exploding fuel, sank around a kilometre from where it had struck the mine. A month later the armistice was signed and as far as Sardinia was concerned the war was over.
(Historical research by Gianpaolo Porcu)

Diving to the wreck

Your loran gear will take you to the right area and an echo sounding will then identify the location of the wreck. You descend along your line for around 20 metres until the shape of the *Romagna* suddenly appears 15 metres below. She is about 100 metres long and is lying upright on the sand, almost as if she were ready to recommence the voyage. You reach the highest parts of the wreck at a depth of around 32 metres. Virtually all of the deck structures have collapsed, including the great masts and the funnels, and only the lower parts of the cabins remain. You should move towards the stern where the plates appear to be harnessed by myriad lines and ropes: you need to be very careful here to avoid getting caught up. Moving away from the hull slightly, the impression of size increases. If you descend to the sea-bed at the

A - The hull of the Romagna *is lying on a sandy sea-bed. Around the prow, hundreds of black brittlestars crawl over the sand in search of food; they are present during the day too.*

B - The imposing stern of the Romagna *looms suddenly out of the blue. The wreck is lying upright and, using the diver as a reference, you get a good idea of its size from this photograph.*

C - The propeller has a diameter of around 4 metres and the rudder is over 5 metres tall. The intensity of the light is a clear indication of the depth: over 40 metres.

stern, a further 10 metres down, the sight of the enormous propeller and rudder alone is worth making the dive for. The blades are longer than a man and the rudder is 5 or 6 metres high. The view from below is spectacular. The wreck is wreathed in a cloud of Anthias, whilst the sandy bottom is carpeted with black brittlestars. As you make your way back to the deck it is difficult to work out just what the distorted metalwork once was and what it looked like. You need to make many dives to gain a good overall picture of the wreck.

Tall sargasso weeds, some reaching 50 cm, are growing on the plates, and occasionally a large school of sea breams passes by, and many scorpionfish lie motionless, waiting to pounce. Large congers and moray eels hide out in the pipework and amidst the wreckage. An anchor of respectable size is still attached to a deck bulkhead, whilst further forward you will come across a bathtub. What it is doing there is anybody's guess. Perhaps the cabin which once housed it was a bathroom ripped apart in the explosion; what is certain is that there are no longer any walls or a ceiling. The left flank of the ship appears to be bulging: the explosions and the fire probably distorted the plates. The tall masts are now lying on the deck, and the one at the prow has fallen into the great gash caused by mine. At the point of impact, on the port side of the prow, the ripped and twisted plates provide eloquent testimony to the violence of the explosion. In contrast, the starboard side appears to have been cut off cleanly. There are scattered heaps of material on the sand in front of the wreck which are partially buried and difficult to identify. Here again a concentration of black brittlestars covers the sea-bed. The bow section is too far from the rest of the hull to be reached during the dive, but if it were possible it would not be difficult to find. A long trail of wreckage and fragments seems to be trying to maintain contact between the two parts of the ship. You need to make a second dive to find the bow section, and it is like diving to a whole new wreck. It lies at a depth of 43 metres amidst a cloud of red

damselfish. There are certain clues which confirm that this is indeed the bow of the *Romagna*.

Again the port side is distorted with the shattered plates indicating the point of impact with the mine. The starboard side might have been cut with an oxy-acetylene flame and the anchor is still attached to a large chain. A couple of metres away a large moray eel has made its home between the plates. The small section of surviving deck is covered with wood, as is that of the main section of the wreck. I saw a school of big sea breams swimming inside. As with all wrecks, the *Romagna* will provide you with something new each time you visit her.

D - Close to the stemrail, the deck is covered with equipment and wreckage that is hard to identify. You can make out the form of a small derrick that was probably mounted on a rotating platform.

E - A cloud of Anthias surrounds the stern of the Romagna close to the mooring bollards, today encrusted with sponges, algae and numerous other organisms. The ship is draped with countless lines and cables abandoned by fishermen; divers must therefore be very careful to avoid getting entangled.

F - The prow of the Romagna was ripped off by the explosion of a mine, and is now to be found around 800 metres from the rest of the hull. The chain bearing the large Hall anchor hangs from the starboard side.

AMERIQUE
by Roberto Rinaldi

AMERIQUE

SICILY
(ITALY)

CALABRIA
(ITALY)

Torre
Faro

Strait of Messina

MESSINA

SCILLA

REGGIO
CALABRIA

Capo
dell'Armi

FRANCE

ITALY

MEDITERRANEAN
SEA

RATINGS

Location difficulty: minimum.
Visibility: usually very good.
Currents: often strong.
Diving difficulty: high.
Lines and nets: none.
Historical interest: average.
Photographic interest: high.
Biological interest: high.

DATA FILE

Type of wreck: merchant ship.
Nationality: British.
Date of construction:
        early 19th century.
Tonnage: unknown.
Date of sinking: perhaps 1910.
Cause of sinking: unknown.
Localisation: not far from Torre Faro.
Distance from shore:
        about 150 metres.
Minimum depth: 35 metres.
Maximum depth: 68 metres.

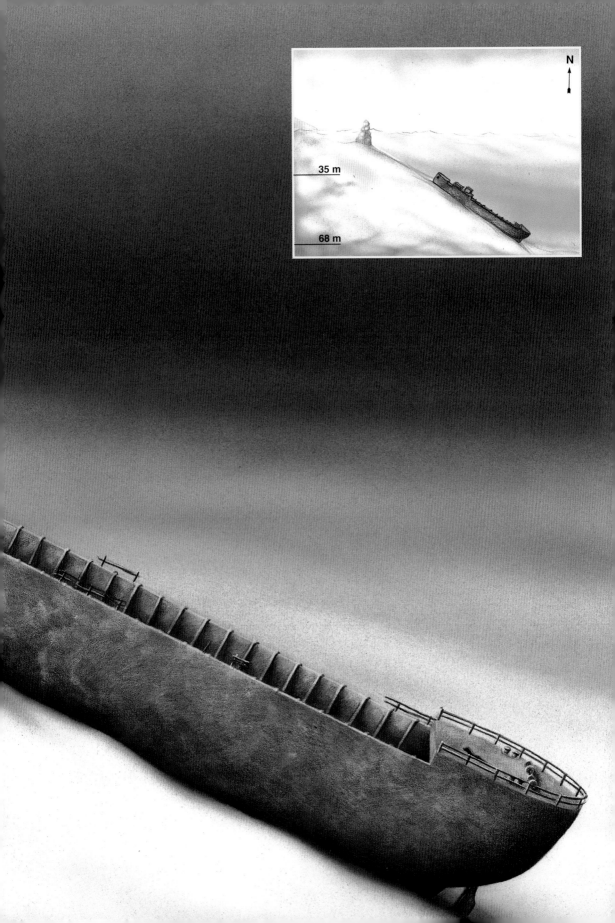

35 m

68 m

N

THE AMERIQUE

Little is known for sure about this elegant old ship lying in front of Torre Faro, at the extreme Northern end of the Sicilian side of the Strait of Messina.
The tales passed on by the older generation talk about a ship beached at Torre Faro at the turn of the century which was then dragged to the bottom by the currents. The present position of the ship would seem to lend weight to this theory, although it has to be said that it is a characteristic common to most of the wrecks in the Strait of Messina to have first run aground and then slipped into the depths. It is only normal that the captain of a ship in difficulties should head towards a nearby sandy coast .
A chart from the era portrays a steamship with its prow emerging from the water just in front of the village of Torre Faro and names it as the *Amerique*. This is all that we have managed to find out about this ship to date, but it is still a splendid wreck to explore, even though the difficulty of the dive makes it suitable only for experts.

Diving to the wreck

It is fairly easy to localise the site: you dive from the shore, entering the water protected by a breakwater directly in front of the trattoria "da Minico il pescatore" at Torre Faro, not far from the tall pylon marking the tip of Sicily. Take great care!!! The currents in the area can be violent and it is thus indispensable to seek the advice of the local experts or the diving centres operating in the area who will be able to provide you with the exact timetable of the slack water, when the direction of the current is reversed.
The timetable can be worked out with a fair degree of precision from the tide tables, but you need to know how to interpret these on the basis of the numerous variables applying to each different point of the Strait.

A - An old postcard is the only clue we have to the name of the wreck: Amerique.

B - In the limpid waters of the Strait of Messina, the juxtaposition of a diver reveals the notable dimensions of the prow of the steamer. The currents have dug away the sand and the hull appears to be "hovering" over the bottom.

C - Trying to reach the stern is most unwise as it is lying at a depth of 68 metres; moreover the area is frequently affected by potentially very strong currents.

Even after carefully studying the tables you can easily be caught out by an unexpected current and should bear this in mind when planning your dive, and also when assessing your own abilities prior to tackling such a demanding descent. Finding the wreck is very easy: all you need to do is enter the water directly in front of the trattoria and descend to the tip of the concrete block breakwater. You follow a sandy slope, typical of the Strait of Messina, taking care to head southwards.

A deep channel in the sediment dug by the current intercepted by the large ship will help you to find the wreck. Your first impression of the ship lying upright on the sea-bed

is truly stunning: the gigantic prow looms threateningly over you, suspended over the sandy bottom which is unceasingly scoured by the action of the current. At this point you are at a depth of about 40 metres, whilst the tip of the prow lies at a little under than 30 metres. Before continuing with a description of the ship, it would be useful to make some observations on how to manage the dive should you be surprised by the current. Usually the flow of water is running parallel to the coast, perpendicular to the wreck.

The hull provides you with an extremely useful shelter, especially as the flanks of the ship are very interesting. From here you can move up to the deck and explore the interior of the superstructure, still benefiting from protection from the current. When you come to ascend at the end of the dive you should always follow the sea-bed, and never try to battle against the current which will only take you either to the North or the South of the point of entry to which you can return by swimming at a depth of 3 metres if, as is probable, the water is still and calm at this level. Alternatively, should the current still be strong even this close to the shore you can always return to your starting point by foot along the road. It is worth repeating that under no circumstances should you try to swim against the current. Turning back to the starboard flank of the wreck, you will find it encrusted with beautiful sea-fans, sponges and other benthic organisms even at the shallowest depths at the prow. You could plan your dive to reach a depth of 50 metres, whilst to see the same things on the port side you would have to descend even deeper. Having photographed

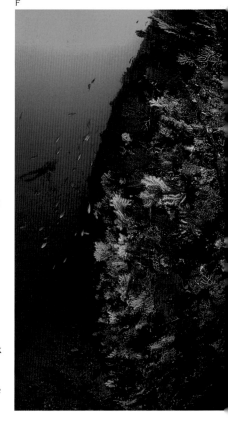

the sea-fans, you should move up to the deck, which is itself rather uninteresting, with its superstructure in fairly poor conditions and its large holds full of sediment. It is, however, worth reaching the centre section of the ship. Here you can see a bathtub in what remains of the cabins on the starboard side. The sight of the wreck from above, lying on the sandy bottom in water of rare clarity, is itself enough to make the dive worthwhile. We would advise you not to dive deeper than the remains of the cabins, even though the stern is impressive. The bottom lies at 68 metres which is really is too deep. From the cabins you should follow the deck towards the bow, swimming on to find the channel in the sand which you follow up to the decompression depths. Should you be caught out by the current, you should shelter behind the flank of the ship and ascend along the sea-bed, without resisting the flow pushing you in one direction or the other.

D - There are a number of cabins in the centre section of the ship, but these have suffered considerable damage whilst the ship has been lying on the sea-bed. The only point of interest inside them is an old bath-tub which can still be seen.

E - There is also a very small structure closer to the prow. This probably housed storerooms for ropes and other equipment.

F - The most incredible and spectacular feature of the wreck of the Amerique is the dense covering of benthic organisms completely covering both flanks.

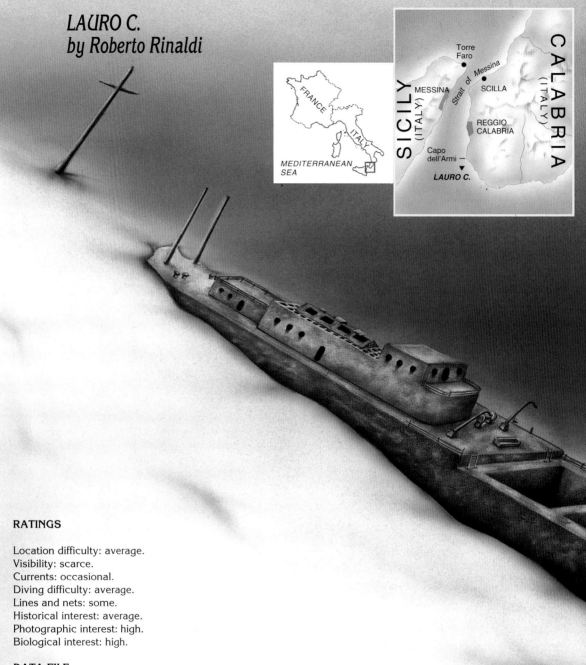

LAURO C.
by Roberto Rinaldi

FRANCE
ITALY
MEDITERRANEAN SEA

SICILY (ITALY)
CALABRIA (ITALY)
Torre Faro
Strait of Messina
MESSINA
SCILLA
REGGIO CALABRIA
Capo dell'Armi
LAURO C.

RATINGS

Location difficulty: average.
Visibility: scarce.
Currents: occasional.
Diving difficulty: average.
Lines and nets: some.
Historical interest: average.
Photographic interest: high.
Biological interest: high.

DATA FILE

Type of wreck: merchant ship.
Nationality: Italian.
Date of construction: unknown.
Tonnage: unknown.
Date of sinking: 1941.
Cause of sinking: torpedo.
Localisation: one kilometre south
        of Capo dell'Armi.
Distance from shore:
        about 100 metres.
Minimum depth: about 27 metres.
Maximum depth: about 57 metres.

27 m

57 m

N

THE LAURO C.

He was born at Licata in Sicily in 1913, but since the summer of 1941, the ex-navy diver Ferdinando Todaro has lived in a house close Capo dell'Armi on the Calabrian shore of the Strait of Messina.

His destiny was linked to that of an attractive ship, the *Lauro C.*, fatally damaged during the Second World War.

The adventure of the Lauro and the unwitting diver began in late spring, 1941 at Trieste, where the ship began loading munitions destined to supply the Italian troops fighting in North Africa. The holds were stocked with explosives, telephone cabling, vehicle parts and also wine, beer and perfume, goods of limited value to the men fighting a desert war.

In the summer the *Lauro C.* left Trieste, sailed the length of the Adriatic and headed West with the intention of passing through the Strait of Messina and joining a convoy bound for Africa. Unfortunately she was still on her own when she was spotted by a British submarine and torpedoed at the very entrance to the Strait, almost within sight of her destination.

A crew member was killed in the engine room and the rudder was damaged by the explosion. The ship began to circle helplessly until a tow line was hooked up and she was put aground on a pebbled beach half a mile from Capo dell'Armi. The ship's misfortunes did not end here, as she was beached at a point where a stream met the sea and she was slowly dragged towards the sea-bed. Ferdinando Todaro was called after the attack and charged with the task of recovering the cargo.

Don Ferdinando proudly showed us his Diver's Handbook, the text book from the Varignano school he attended in 1933, and his leather boots with their lead weights.

A - Flicking through Don Ferdinando's old photo album we found a shot of the prow of the Lauro C. from the time when it still emerged above the surface of the water. Three years later this section also sank and is now buried under the sand on the sea-bed.

B - Don Ferdinando at around thirty years of age, posing for the photographer alongside his assistants before a dive.

C - Don Ferdinando still proudly keeps his helmet, lead boots, waterproofed canvas suit, work permit and diving school text book.

"The ship remained with her prow out of the water for two years before disappearing", he told us, "but no.1 and no.2 holds were already underwater. Today they are below the sand, buried by the sediment, and marked only by a metal mast emerging for a few metres and the diver's tales. These were the holds containing the flasks of Chianti and the cases of beer. Don Ferdinando stopped off here before every deep dive, recovered a case of wine or beer and sent it up to the men in the cover boat who as well as following his movements were responsible for operating the hand-pumped air compressor: "You should have seen how they pumped afterwards!".

Diving to the wreck

Proceeding along the sandy slope beyond the beach you find the first structures which really emerge from the sands.
You can enter the engine room though a skylight.
It makes a convenient entrance which leads into a large area in which you should use your buoyancy jacket to allow you to hover. "The entrance into the *Lauro C.*'s engine room was difficult for us", says Don Ferdinando, "it was tricky passing through the half-open hatches and then lowering yourself down, with a jump of around 10 metres through open water, with lead-weighted shoes and a copper helmet."
Whilst he was speaking the diver caressed the helmet with a still sure hand. The helmet was attached via a bayonet fitting to a metal collar which was in turn attached to the diving suit, and was in place via a lever.
One day the men forgot to lock this lever and Ferdinando dived to the sea-bed and suddenly found himself without his helmet.
He had his head underwater, could not see anything and of course could no longer breathe the air from the tube attached to his helmet which had finished up who knows where. As if this was not enough, his problems were compounded by the lead weights

D - During the descent you pass the first buried holds and, below the sediment, you can make out the superstructure of the ship. In this photograph you can clearly see the engine-room access hatches.

E - In this shot you can see the deepest parts of the wreck worth visiting; the divers are swimming over the stern. Beyond the ship's rail, the sea-bed lies at a depth of 57 metres and it really is not worth descending that far

F - There are a number of winches to be seen on the deck of the Lauro *C. close to the holds. Presumably steel cables would once have led from the winches to the mast via a block and tackle and down into the hold where they would be hooked up to the goods to be unloaded.*

on his chest and boots.
Instinctively he threw his head
down, dumped the ballast and
the air trapped in the suit pulled
him to the surface where
fortunately he avoided colliding
with the cover boat and was
dragged on board. "As a
punishment I refused to bring up
another bottle for a whole month!"
Once you have passed through
the entrance to the engine room
you will find a number of cabins
with doors facing towards the
stern. These can also be entered
if you are careful.
A number of large capstans
precede the first of the large holds
which can be visited: at this point
the deck is at a depth of 35
metres, and it would be as well to
consult your pressure gauge and
dive computer before entering the
hold which is at least 7 or 8
metres deeper and full of fine
mud. Mud was already a problem
for Don Ferdinando who told us
that visibility was zero after a few
minutes work. "But I'm very good
with explosives: it needed just two
charges on the flanks of the ship
to allow the current to pass
through and clear away the
sediment."
A bulkhead divides the first hold
from the next, beyond which you
can see the tall mast, the symbol
of this ship. It was probably used
as a derrick for loading and
unloading the cargo.
Today you will find it encrusted
with marine organisms, in
particular you should look out
for a splendid colony of unusually
large white colonial cnidarians
covering the metal at a depth
of 20 metres.
There are always many fish
around the mast, some of them
large examples.
Don Ferdinando also saw many
fish during his dives, "there were
often very large sharks and
hammerheads.
They never bothered me, but had
me worried all the same".
The base of the mast lies at a
depth of 42 metres and another
two large capstans face the
opening of another hold.
On the bottom, at 50 metres,
you will find many bottles

A

B

C

A - Two symmetrical
sets of steps - you
can see one in the
photograph - lead to
the poop deck.

B - A diver is
exploring the
hatches which
cover the engine-
room. It is possible
to reach the interior
from here.
The entrance is
fairly easy and the
exit is always in
sight once you are
inside.

C - The tall mast is
the symbol of this
wreck. Encrusted
with marine
organisms, it is
constantly
surrounded by a
cloud of Anthias
and colonised by
gigantic white
cnidarians.

D - This photograph
portrays a capstan
located on the rim
of the hold. In the
background you
can see the form
of the large mast.

D

of Campari. Coming out of the hold you reach the stern castle. It would be possible to enter some of the cabins here, but you should not forget that you are at 45 metres and you have a long swim to reach the decompression depths close to the shore. Looking over the rail at the stern you will see the sandy bottom at 57 metres, with the propellers buried in the sediment. Ferdinando Todaro looks out at the sea from the balcony of his home, a few hundred metres from the wreck. He half closes his eyes as he searches through his memories. Then he smiles "From that day on I stayed because a woman hooked me".

E

G

F

E - It is easy for modern divers with aqualungs to reach the skylight and descend into the engine-room; it was less so for divers in the past, weighed down with kilos of lead who had to make the jump with the risk that their air hoses might get caught up, turning the interior into a deadly trap.

F - A diver inspecting the last hold, the deepest of the series at around 50 metres. Here you will find great quantities of bottles of Campari.

G - This shot clearly illustrates the steps leading to the poop deck.

168 - A diver isobserving one of the four engines of the B-17 that was ditched off Calvi on the 14th of February, 1944. The four engines are still in place but some of the propeller blades have been removed.